"Feeling anxious is so much a part of modern life that we almost forget how limiting it can be. But not these authors. They offer us clear information and techniques for dealing with anxiety on a daily basis. They teach us what the brain does when we are anxious, and what we can do about it, by changing the focus of our thinking and getting us on the yoga mat and meditation cushion for time-honored practices.

"But mostly they give us readers the confidence that we can transcend our anxiety and lead richer and more enjoyable lives. Highly recommended for yoga teachers and others interested in the whole picture of anxiety, including the spiritual angst that usually accompanies it. I especially enjoyed the personal stories scattered throughout the book."

> —Judith Hanson Lasater, Ph.D., PT, has been teaching yoga since 1971 and is author of eight books, including *Yogabody*

"Writing in a clear, step-by-step format, Mary and Rick NurrieStearns provide simple practices to help identify and counteract negative thoughts, induce relaxation, develop awareness, reduce stress, and heal anxiety. The authors create a connection with the reader by using images and examples from everyday life that resonate with everyone's experiences. *Yoga for Anxiety* integrates modern psychology with basic yoga practices, including postures, breathing, mindfulness, and meditation. In the early chapters, basic information suitable for beginners provides the foundation for more advanced material as the book progresses. For anyone suffering from anxiety, *Yoga for Anxiety* is a great place to begin the journey to recovery."

> —Patricia L. Gerbarg, MD, and Richard P. Brown, MD, coauthors of *How to Use Herbs, Nutrients, and Yoga in Mental Health Care*

"Yoga is one of the best-validated therapies in the entire field of integrative medicine. It is especially valuable because it addresses all we are: body, mind, and spirit. *Yoga for Anxiety* is an excellent guide for anyone seeking greater serenity, peace, and fulfillment—and who isn't?"

—Larry Dossey, MD, author of *Healing Words* and *The Power of Premonitions*

"By combining traditional psychology with the deep teachings of yoga, Mary and Rick NurrieStearns help you move past anxiety in order to experience your true nature. *Yoga for Anxiety* clearly shows that when you are willing to mindfully face and release your anxiety, it actually becomes a doorway to deep inner freedom and happiness."

—Michael A. Singer, author of *The Untethered Soul*

yoga for anxiety

meditations and practices for calming the body and mind

Mary NurrieStearns, LCSW, RYT
Rick NurrieStearns

New Harbinger Publications, Inc.

Publisher's Note

This publication is designed to provide accurate and authoritative information in regard to the subject matter covered. It is sold with the understanding that the publisher is not engaged in rendering psychological, financial, legal, or other professional services. If expert assistance or counseling is needed, the services of a competent professional should be sought.

Note to the reader

While yoga practices are empowering and safe, they are not substitutes for medical care. Sometimes yoga practices are most effective as supplemental self-care to counseling and medical advice. Professional treatment, including medications, can be helpful, especially if you have a history of trauma or intense anxiety. If you are receiving treatment for anxiety, please consult with your therapist or doctor before doing the practices in this book.

Distributed in Canada by Raincoast Books

Copyright © 2010 by Mary NurrieStearns and Rick NurrieStearns
New Harbinger Publications, Inc.
5674 Shattuck Avenue
Oakland, CA 94609
www.newharbinger.com

FSC
Mixed Sources
Product group from well-managed
forests and other controlled sources
Cert no. SW-COC-002283
www.fsc.org
© 1996 Forest Stewardship Council

Cover design by Amy Shoup
Text design by Michele Waters-Kermes
Acquired by Jess O'Brien
Edited by Nelda Street

Printed in the United States of America

Library of Congress Cataloging-in-Publication Data

NurrieStearns, Mary.
  Yoga for anxiety : meditations and practices for calming the body and mind / Mary NurrieStearns and Rick NurrieStearns.
    p. cm.
  Includes bibliographical references.
  ISBN-13: 978-1-57224-651-5 (pbk. : alk. paper)
  ISBN-10: 1-57224-651-0 (pbk. : alk. paper) 1. Stress management. 2. Yoga. 3. Anxiety. I. NurrieStearns, Rick, 1953- II. Title.
  RA785.N87 2010
  616.9'8--dc22

                              2009044376

12   11   10

10   9   8   7   6   5   4   3   2   1   First printing

contents

acknowledgments

We thank New Harbinger Publications, especially Jess O'Brien for making this book possible, Jess Beebe for being a guiding light that kept our writing on course, and Nelda Street for excellent copyediting.

We give special thanks to our writing consultant Hal Zina Bennett, who helped us express our hearts in this book—and a whole lot more.

We thank our clients, students, and retreatants. Your courage to stay the course touches our hearts and deepens our appreciation for how powerful these practices are.

We thank Sara Wright for beautifully modeling the yoga poses for the photos in this book, and Chris Claussen for taking great photographs. We thank Mary's yoga students for helping to develop the sequence for daily practice.

We thank those who have inspired us along the way, including Gay and Kathlyn Hendricks, Father Thomas Keating, Richard Moss, John Tarrant, Adyashanti, Pema Chödrön, Hameed Ali, and Eckhart Tolle.

We thank our cats, who purred us along, and our dog, who made sure we took breaks to walk.

And we thank our family and friends, who waited patiently for us to be available again.

—Rick and Mary

introduction

Many years ago, we hiked a beautiful trail in Utah's Zion National Park, called Angels Landing. The trail started off with a strenuous hike up a number of switchbacks on a paved path. After topping the paved switchbacks, we entered a canyon with a gradually inclining, shaded path. Just as we thought we were nearing the end of the trail, the trail turned and revealed that we had even steeper switchbacks ahead of us. We were determined to reach the top of the trail, because descending hikers seemed thrilled to have experienced its breathtaking view and we wanted to see what everyone was talking about.

The path became increasingly intimidating and scary. Heavy chains were bolted into the rock walls to hang on to. On the edge of a cliff, the trail was only a foot wide with a sheer 1,200 foot drop to the river below. Hikers on their way back down encouraged us to go on, declaring that the view from the top was marvelous. Sustained by their support, we continued. We haltingly climbed the same way everybody does, putting one foot down in front of the other and going breath by breath by breath. Once we reached the summit, we smiled and breathed sighs of relief, yet we both knew that we had to go back down the same way we had come up. We worried our way through our lunch and then began the return trip. During our descent, there were moments when we focused more on what might go wrong and less on where the ground was solid beneath our feet. We had to stop from time to time, remind each other to breathe, remember that we were okay, and then begin again.

Sometime after our Zion trip, Rick resolved to walk through the forest near our home as a daily meditation. Having long relied on his steadfast and steely mind to get him through life, he sometimes found that it cut him off from his aliveness. Putting one foot in front of the other helped Rick slow down and connect to himself, which propelled him into a powerful healing journey because he was then better able to feel and be touched by the meditative practices he had done for many years.

Taking one step at a time has helped enable Mary to live inside of herself. Her thoughts used to race ahead of her body, worrying about what would happen next and what she needed to take care of. It was as if her mind lived in a different time zone than her body. After the Angels Landing hike, she silently recited the words, "Step here," during her morning walks, because it focused her attention on walking as she walked. Gradually her body and mind started moving together as one, making it possible for her to integrate what her yoga practices revealed to her.

Putting one foot in front of the other is so simple that it can become mechanical, allowing our minds to go elsewhere and be out of sync with our experience. As a consequence, we forget what we're doing, who we are, and where we are. All this forgetting causes painful anxiety. Healing ourselves from this anxiety depends on our remembering again.

We've been on a yoga journey together since we met, twenty years ago, and this book is our way of sharing what we've learned. We've both suffered from anxiety and found that yoga practices help us to remember who we are, to connect to ourselves, and to engage more fully in life. We don't claim scholarly knowledge about yoga, but we've experienced its real and lasting benefits. Yoga has brought profound healing to us and to the people we work with in retreats, seminars, and counseling.

While yoga practices are empowering and safe, they are not substitutes for medical care. Sometimes yoga practices are most effective as supplemental self-care to counseling and medical advice. Professional treatment, including medications, can be helpful, especially if you have a history of trauma or intense anxiety. If you're receiving treatment for anxiety, please consult with your therapist or doctor before doing the practices in this book.

We teach only what we personally practice, so know that we're with you as you try the practices covered in this book. And along the way, remember to go step by step—breath by breath by breath.

chapter 1

understanding anxiety

Difficulties are soul shaping.... They can be lessons that lead us to know who we are...

—Jean Shinoda Bolen, MD

anxiety is a great struggle, one that can follow you around for years and, at times, feel unbearable. And yet, amazingly, with the help of yoga practices, anxiety is not only tolerable; it decreases and becomes much less of an influence in your life. It's also one of those difficulties that, when embraced and seen into, can show you who you truly are. And if it does, it gives you the gift of a lifetime. As odd as this sounds, you're about to discover that anxiety is not the adversary that it feels like.

Know that, as someone who suffers from anxiety, you're not alone. Many people have endured it, ourselves included, and it's not a personal flaw to be anxious. We live in stressful times. Economic upheaval, terrorism, and global warming threaten our collective existence. Even though your anxiety feels personal and is related to your individual experiences, it occurs in the context of local, national, and global anxiety. We don't know how to resolve the collective anxiety, but the many yoga practices discussed in this book can help you unwind and access inner peace. We also know, from our own experience, that reducing anxiety brings joy to your life and encourages those around you. So as you focus on your individual healing, take comfort in knowing that your healing touches the lives of others in a positive way.

This book isn't just about anxiety; it's fundamentally about learning to be calm and contented. Although you've experienced anxiety, you've probably also been relaxed, even if some time has passed since you felt that way. We're inclined toward relaxation because it's a natural state, one wherein we connect to ourselves and don't struggle with life. Being relaxed doesn't make you passive, uninvolved, or irresponsible. Rather, it allows you to enjoy your life and feel okay being you. At the same time, it helps make you sane and enables you to make wise choices. Practice by practice, step by step, moment by moment, yoga helps you to know who you are and be more at ease in your life.

Mary has a long history with anxiety, and attributes much of her healing to yoga. These practices continue to steady and calm her when needed, as the following story highlights. Mary used to have panic attacks when flying commercially, so she was surprised many years ago, when we first met, that she loved flying with Rick in a single-engine airplane. Mary recalls:

Early on in our relationship, I fell in love with Rick when he took me flying in a private airplane. He was so happy up in the sky, dancing with the clouds. Then, shortly after our marriage, our finances changed and we no longer had the extra money for an airplane. For years Rick wistfully watched as airplanes flew overhead. A couple of years ago, our economic situation improved. One day Rick telephoned me from work and said, "Hey Mary, I found a great deal on an airplane." I shuddered with fear and answered coolly, "What do we need an airplane for?" Rick's voice fell, and he muttered, "Okay." A month later, he called and excitedly said, "The price for the airplane has dropped substantially; it's a super deal now." Knowing that he loved flying, I swallowed my fear and responded, "If you want to buy the airplane, do it with my blessings." What I hadn't told Rick was that I was concerned about being safe in the plane.

I figured we would be safer in the plane if I also knew how to fly, so Rick is teaching me. While learning to fly, I've felt intense anxiety and even had a couple of mild panic attacks, the first in over twenty-five years. However, thanks to my yoga practices, I was able to breathe deeply, focus on what I was doing, and witness my worrisome thoughts. As a result, the panic didn't totally overwhelm me. Embracing anxiety and breathing through it gives me confidence, and now I'm sometimes relaxed while flying the plane. Additionally, sharing Rick's enjoyment of flying is wonderful for me, and he's profoundly touched that I'm facing my old fear of falling to my death.

Experiencing fear and anxiety is uncomfortable, and if you're like most people, you try to avoid both. You become resistant to experiencing them, wish they would go away, and don't want to know them better or deal with them. Yet, intimately knowing anxiety helps to dispel it, and this book shows you how to safely and gradually heal your anxiety. This first chapter contains a lot of information about anxiety, because we've found that learning more about it is a good first step in healing from it.

distinguishing between fear and anxiety

So that you can really understand what's going on inside you, let's differentiate between the words "fear" and "anxiety," because they're often used interchangeably. Fear is the physical response to an external threat. It's an instinctual, life-preserving response to danger. Anxiety is not a response to imminent danger. It's associated with memories of fear, anticipation of fear, and perhaps a biological predisposition to being anxious.

How anxiety actually happens in our bodies is amazing and intricate. According to Joseph LeDoux in his article, "Emotional Memory" (2007), emotional experiences leave strong traces in our brains. Through a process called *fear conditioning*, cells that process and transmit information in the nervous system become conditioned, encoding the memory of fear and enabling fear to take on a life of its own in our bodies and minds. Thus, thinking about a past frightening event triggers the fear response in the present to some degree. For example, when you merely remember a time when you were too close to a sheer drop-off, you feel the fear just as you did when you were actually there.

Fear

You know how debilitating fear can be. Being faced with something you really fear leaves you feeling immobilized, stopped in your tracks. Generally you avoid what you fear, whether it's spiders, snakes, heights, flying, crowds, closed spaces, public speaking, being alone, or countless other experiences. Fear can prevent you from doing something you really want to do. For instance, if you're afraid of heights and find yourself on the observation deck of a tall building or at the Grand Canyon, where you want to step up to the handrail to take a look, you hesitate, swallow, and feel your heart beating. You stand back and marvel at, and perhaps even feel jealous of, those who go to the edge. Or, maybe you tighten, muster your courage, and step up. Either way, you're in the grip of fear, which infuses you with unpleasant sensations that pervade your experience of that moment.

The inclination to stand back is reflexive and consists of a cluster of activities that includes vision changes, hormonal reactions, physical responses, thoughts, and behaviors. Viewing a sheer drop from its apex causes a complex process to take place within you in a fraction of a second. You become aware; you get a jolt of energy, and your body freezes. Seemingly in the same flash, you respond by thinking, *yikes*! After retreating or forcing yourself to go forward, you may feel your heart pound and your hands tremble.

You've felt fear and how its residual effects endure. Fear leaves an imprint, a form of physical conditioning that you consciously and unconsciously store in your brain. After being in a situation that frightened you, related stimuli can reengage the whole fear response. In that way, fear lives on inside you.

Impending danger triggers a response in the brain and the body, one that's hardwired and designed to preserve life. Called the *fight-or-flight* response, it enables you to run or take other action to save your life. This is an instinctual, hormonal process that we have in common with the animal kingdom. Rather than being solely a psychological response, it's a complex neurophysiological response involving several organs and areas of the brain.

Anxiety

Your experience of anxiety is the result of a looping dialogue among a mind preoccupied with safety, nerve cells that interpret life in the present moment as being more dangerous than it is, and a body that revs up to run away or stand its ground. Here's why it may seem that you not only fight anxiety but experience it as a losing battle. The part of your brain that processes fear can't tell whether fear originates from your thoughts or from some real physical threat. Either way, your brain triggers the fight-or-flight response. In other words, your body reacts to danger, real or imagined, in the only way it knows how: with a big charge of energy that prepares it to protect your life. And, you aren't even aware of what's happening, since this occurs in the unconscious mind!

Revving up, your body then fuels your fearful thoughts. It's as if your body provides evidence to your thoughts that there's something to be stressed about. The responses of the body and the mind amplify one another, and in that way, anxiety is not only heightened but also perpetuated. This leaves you in a state of distress, even when, in reality, there's no actual threat to your survival! Hopefully, this little discussion helps you appreciate why anxiety is so uncomfortable. When anxiety is a mystery, it can be daunting to deal with, but knowing about anxiety actually increases the effectiveness of the practices we teach in this book to alleviate it.

the facets of anxiety

Anxiety has five facets:

- The habit of avoidance

- An out-of-balance body

- Relived trauma

- The belief that something is wrong with you

- The mighty current

Let's explore them so you can recognize which of its aspects pertain to your experience of anxiety.

Habit of Avoidance

One facet of anxiety is the habit of avoidance. The greatest fear is that of fear itself. Even the idea of being afraid is paralyzing: *I would be too terrified; I couldn't do it. No, I won't even consider doing that! That would scare me to death! I'm afraid it might hurt.* When Mary resisted the idea of buying an airplane, she was motivated by avoidance.

The discomfort anxiety arouses is a powerful motivator, driving your choice to stay safe rather than take a risk. You probably know this yourself, because most of us attempt to avoid experiencing anxiety. However, avoiding anxiety can rob you of developing your potential and of living life fully. When your perceived need to stay safe is paramount, life shrinks, reducing to risk avoidance and needing to be in control.

Body Out of Balance

Another facet of anxiety, a state of bodily imbalance, is when anxiety stems from physiological causes. Disturbances in the brain's chemical messengers and changing hormones in women's monthly cycles are two biological causes. Inner-ear disturbances and a prolapsed mitral valve in the heart, causing what's known as "heart murmurs," may also cause anxiety.

Additionally, the body is sensitive to what goes in it. What you ingest can cause anxiety. Caffeine, alcohol, nicotine, prescription drugs, cold remedies, decongestants, diet pills, and certain recreational drugs can cause anxiety.

Relived Trauma

Another facet of anxiety is relived trauma. When reliving trauma becomes chronic, it's medically defined as *post-traumatic stress disorder*. If you're one of the millions of people who have suffered past trauma, you may unconsciously re-create the fear response when some of your nerve cells interpret what's happening in your life today as the old trauma, and signal your brain to prepare your body to defend itself. This communication occurs outside of your conscious control, which means that when this happens, you aren't intentionally doing something wrong and you aren't thinking your way into anxiety.

Trauma lives on in your body; it becomes a familiar experience, just the way it is for your body. Trauma may perpetuate itself through addiction to adrenalin, which can lead you to participate in dangerous, slightly risky, or dramatic behaviors (such as gambling, promiscuous sex, violence, or driving dangerously) for the sake of the adrenalin rush that such experiences produce. When the fear response feels normal, even desirable, to you, you'll seek it out through such risky activities.

Trauma also lives on through thinking self-deprecating thoughts and acting on destructive impulses, which can show up as poor personal hygiene, hanging out with people who aren't good for you, using self-talk that puts you down, and engaging in a multitude of other injurious behaviors. These behaviors unwittingly re-create the effects of trauma, thus feeding the fear response and maintaining a painful, vicious cycle.

Something's Wrong with Me

Another facet of anxiety is believing that something's wrong with you. This aspect of anxiety stems from misunderstanding who you are. It's a case of mistaken identity. You think you're imperfect, somehow flawed. This facet of anxiety is rooted in beliefs and ideas about who you are as a human being. Here, it *is* your thinking that causes anxiety, even though you may not be aware that you even have these thoughts. "I am not okay" is a bedrock belief that fuels the growth of thoughts about being incapable, for example, *I could never do that*, and being unlovable, for example, *If I disagree, he won't like me and may even abandon me*. These thoughts keep you in the grip of fear, distorting your experience of life.

These distorting thoughts live in the recesses of your mind. Buried in the subconscious, they can originate at any time of life, although we most often associate them with chronic or acute childhood trauma or neglect. Because trauma can be so devastating to our bodies and minds, adult traumas can have the same effect as childhood traumas. When you bring these thoughts into consciousness (we show you how to compassionately do this) and see them for what they are, these false perceptions lose their power as unconscious motivators.

The gross misunderstanding of who you are is a powerful cause of anxiety that's covered in much detail later on in this book. For now, we're merely introducing this facet of anxiety along with the other facets.

The Mighty Current

This facet of anxiety, the mighty current, is a strong under-current of anxiety that's difficult to categorize. A powerful energy, it pulls you under and you feel as though you might die. It feels similar to a panic attack yet has a different quality. Panic is heart pounding, breathtaking, raw terror that's time limited. This feels like a relentless current that sucks you under. Immense, it may rise up out of the collective unconscious, ancestral cellular memory, a past life, *kundalini* (energy of consciousness that affects us psychologically and spiritually), societal anxiety, or some combination of these.

This powerful anxiety seems to rise up of its own accord. Not easily accounted for, it seems to accompany midlife crisis, true questions of meaning and existence, and the deepening spiritual journey. It can show up during times of vulnerability, such as physical illness and personal upheaval. This facet of anxiety isn't easily articulated yet needs to be named. If you've felt this current of anxiety, you know it. This is the anxiety that takes you to the floor, where all you can do is breathe, stay conscious, and surrender.

Name Your Facet of Anxiety

As you read through the facets, if you were able to identify the type of anxiety you normally experience, you may find it helpful to give it a name. If your anxiety seems too confusing or overwhelming, then come back to this later if you like. The idea here is to look at your anxiety and get to know it. You may recognize all five facets in yourself, but one may predominate. If you identify a dominant facet, give it a name.

One friend named hers "My Dearest." Her anxiety was excruciating, although familiar and even "normal" for her. It had been with her for as long as she could remember. At age fifty, after her mother's death, she felt safe enough to look into her anxiety. Surrounded by the support of yoga classes, prayer, writing, meditation, and soothing yogic practices, she looked into this facet and identified it as relived trauma.

If you give your anxiety a name, be gentle and understanding. Remember, truth and compassion are very healing. When you truly become acquainted with your facet of anxiety, your heart will melt. Clearly, you didn't intend or desire to be anxious. When you see how it came to be, you see into yourself and your life. You literally become more transparent to yourself, and such clarity is healing.

In summary, anxiety can manifest itself and be experienced in different ways. It tends to become chronic and take on a life of its own. The effects of anxiety can range from mild to severe but take a heavy toll on the body and mind, eroding the quality of your life.

incidence of anxiety

As someone who suffers from anxiety, you may feel isolated. So that you realize how much company you have, let's look at the statistics. The numbers vary, but they all indicate that anxiety is pervasive in this country. In 2005 R. C. Kessler and colleagues reported that approximately forty million American adults aged eighteen and older, or slightly over 18 percent of people in this age group in a given year, have a diagnosable anxiety disorder (Kessler et al. 2005). That's nearly one out of five people. Some people are anxious and don't know it. When it becomes chronic, you can get so used to it that it feels normal. Additionally, many people find ways to function in spite of anxiety. Highly anxious people may even appear to the outside world as calm and contented. Numerous people have said to us, "Nobody has a clue that I'm this anxious."

You and Anxiety

Even though anxiety is definable and diagnosable, it remains a personalized experience. Your anxiety is unique to you and you experience it in your own way. Physically, you may have muscular tension, exhaustion, an upset stomach, and a pounding heart. Or maybe you experience mental symptoms, such as persistent worry, racing thoughts, and distressing images, or have flashbacks of painful scenes. Maybe your anxiety manifests on the emotional level, making you feel irritable, overwhelmed, or apprehensive. Or perhaps you startle easily, often scanning the environment and avoiding potentially scary situations. Perhaps you play it safe so you can remain in control and avoid taking risks. Maybe you have irrational fears that limit you. However you experience anxiety, it's what motivated you to pick up this book in search of relief.

neuroscience and anxiety

Let's go into a little science—not too much, just enough to give you a sense of what happens inside you when you're anxious. It will help you understand your body and will give credence to the yoga practices we teach you.

Conscious and Unconscious Memory

A closer look at what happens in your brain can help you appreciate how anxiety is triggered. In *The Emotional Brain*, Joseph LeDoux (1998) wrote that the brain has two memory systems that are activated by traumatic memory. One memory system stores conscious memories about the who, what, where, and when of the event. These are the details you can recall. Neuroscientists believe that these memories are stored primarily in the *hippocampus* (the part of the brain responsible for learning and remembering) and aspects of the temporal lobe of the brain.

The second memory system stores unconscious memories about how your body responded to past experiences, which are processed by the *amygdalae* (which process fear) and the nerves that connect to them. (Remember those nerve cells mentioned earlier in the chapter that process and transmit information?) This is what triggers the *sympathetic nervous system's* (branch of the autonomic nervous system that becomes active during times of stress) fight-or-flight response, which you feel as fear. So as amazing as it sounds, it's not what you consciously remember that causes the heart pounding and adrenaline rush that signal that your body is charged and ready to do battle or run away.

You Can't Talk Your Way Out of Fear

What you consciously recall and what your body remembers about trauma come from different parts of the brain. These different sources of information communicate with each other, but the connections running from the amygdalae (which, as previously mentioned, process fear) to the *cortex* (which thinks and stores memories) are stronger than from the cortex to the amygdalae.

In other words, the unconscious fear message, "Danger! Run for your life!" is not so easily mediated by the reasonable response, "Oh, it's not dangerous after all; there's a fence between you and the growling guard dog." Even though you intellectually know that you're safe, the fear response continues: your hands shake, your heart pounds, and you keep looking behind you to be sure the dog's still safely behind the fence.

As you know, the fear response is fundamental to our survival. Its purpose is to keep you alive. In the brain, the amygdalae have four jobs:

- Receive information from the outside world

- Determine its significance

- Then trigger the fear response, if appropriate

- Send the message of fear to the cortex so you can assess the situation and decide what to do

Once aroused, it seems as if the fight-or-flight response has to work its way out of your system. At the least, the thinking brain, or cortex, with weaker connections to the amygdalae, has great difficulty using reason to diminish intense emotions. This may explain why it's so difficult to diffuse intense fear by telling yourself to calm down or that there's nothing to be afraid of. You can't talk or reason your way out of it.

Extreme Stress and the Brain

In *Psychobiology of Posttraumatic Stress Disorder* (2006), Bessel A. van der Kolk, a researcher on how extreme stress affects the brain, explains how emotions are not the result of conscious choice. The *limbic* brain structures, such as the amygdalae, determine emotions, as well as the importance of what you notice going on around you. If they interpret something you see, hear, or smell as dangerous, the result is an instinctual, hormonal response that sends an alarm message to the brain. While you're not aware that this internal process is going on, you're probably aware of the anxiety that results, unless it's so familiar to you that you're desensitized to it.

Let's look at how flashbacks occur. Each of your amygdala stores memory, and if something reminds it of a past trauma, your body responds in the same way it did during the original event.

This explains why, for the first few months after being rear-ended in a fender bender, you tense up and hold your breath when a car behind you is slow to brake at a stoplight.

Mental images of past traumas we've experienced activate each amygdala, resulting in strong emotion, and suppress each *frontal lobe*, which inhibits emotions and translates experience into words that can be spoken. Sometimes you're flooded with emotions but can't find words to let others know what's going on. An understanding of how the frontal lobe gets suppressed when the amygdala is activated helps to explain why it's so difficult to express what's happening when you're highly upset.

The frontal part of the brain makes sense of feelings and impulses. However, it does not seem to remove them, partly because when we're stressed, the frontal lobe areas receive less blood flow. Only afterward, when you're no longer intensely agitated, does blood flow increase in your frontal lobes, enabling you to make sense of and talk about what you experienced.

the stress response

Though we've already talked about the stress response, we'll define it here briefly so you can compare it to the relaxation response. In 1915 Dr. Walter Cannon coined the term "fight/flight" in his book *Bodily Changes in Pain, Hunger, Fear, and Rage: An Account of Recent Researches into the Function of Emotional Excitement*. This "fight/flight" response is also called the stress response.

Specifically, under stress:

- Your heart beats faster and your muscles tense.

- Your breathing becomes shallow and you start to perspire.

- The flow of blood to your internal organs and extremities decreases.

- The functioning of your immune and digestive systems is inhibited.

When you're anxious, your body mobilizes for action. But with no need to run away, your body remains revved up, in a state of alarm. Our bodies are not designed to function under a constant state of stress. Over time, the effects of the stress response take a toll on your physical health, energy, mood, and general sense of well-being.

the relaxation response

Except when you're in physical danger, your health and sense of well-being depend on your body's relaxation response. Being relaxed is a whole-body experience and was first described by Herbert Benson in his 1976 book, *The Relaxation Response*. The relaxation response reduces the stress response, and, like the stress response, is initiated in the brain.

Specifically, the relaxation response includes the following:

- Your heart rate slows down and your blood pressure stabilizes.

- Your immune system is boosted.

- Your brain waves slow down.

- Your digestive processes normalize.

- Your quality of sleep improves.

- You experience a sense of well-being.

When your body relaxes after you've been chronically tense, you feel like yourself again or discover a new and delightful sense of ease. Your mental functioning improves and you literally "come to your senses"; that is, you become more aware of what you're seeing, hearing, tasting, smelling, and touching. As a result, you can think more clearly, and more accurately take in information from the outside world.

anxiety and brain wave activity

You've undoubtedly had times when your thoughts raced so quickly that they were incomplete, tumbling over one another and jumping all over the place. This happens when you're anxious or really excited, and it tends to wear you out. Your brain's busyness in making thoughts is called *brain wave activity*, and the pace at which you generate thoughts can be measured. Brain wave activity is examined through *EEG (electroencephalograph) testing*. When you're anxious, your thought wave activity is called *beta waves*, because you're producing thoughts at a rhythm of thirteen to thirty cycles per second.

When you're relaxed, your brain wave activity is called *alpha waves*. Thoughts slow down and take on a more coherent rhythm of about eight to twelve cycles per second. As noisy and worried thoughts subside, the mind becomes quiet and you feel contented. Because your mind is less active, you can relate to what's actually going on and you're more present for the current moment, the now.

neuroscience, exercise, and healing

The body and the brain are incredibly sensitive and resilient. They can be damaged by acute or chronic stress, and turn around and heal from its effects. And you can further the healing process along, as you're about to see.

The brain is constantly creating new neurons. In 1998, Fred Gage and colleagues at the Salk Institute for Biological Studies discovered that we human beings are capable of growing new nerve cells throughout life, if we physically exercise (Eriksson et al. 1998). Physical exercise enhances the growth of new brain cells in the hippocampus, which, as mentioned earlier, is the part of the brain that's essential for learning and remembering. This means that exercising, walking, and practicing the physical postures of yoga daily not only work off accumulated stress in your body but also help your brain.

Exercise is a critical aspect of your healing program. Here's why: Research has established that stress can damage the hippocampus. In *Why Zebras Don't Get Ulcers*, Robert Sapolsky (2004) reported that the hippocampus is vulnerable to stress. It has a higher density of receptors for the stress hormone cortisol than almost any other area of the brain. When stress is chronic, your hippocampus begins to shrink. Stress undeniably takes a toll on your body and your brain, but you're not doomed. You can intervene on your own behalf.

meditation is healthy for your brain

Science has made it clear that physical exercise is indeed powerful medicine. However, there's so much more you can do to find comfort and health. Once again, let's look at research to see what it has demonstrated.

In *Beyond Biofeedback* (1977) Elmer and Alyce Green reported on research conducted in 1970 at the Menninger Foundation in Topeka, Kansas, where they studied voluntary control over involuntary states. A yogi, Swami Rama, altered his brain wave patterns upon demand. In meditative states, he voluntarily went from beta brain waves, associated with active thought, to alpha waves, associated with relaxation, to theta waves, generally associated with unconscious states. In other words, he slowed his thinking way down, possibly similar to what you experience in the fleeting moment before sleep.

The Menninger Foundation study of meditative states was not isolated. In 1966 A. Kasamatsu and T. Hirai verified the effect that meditation has on brain wave activity. Their EEG studies of Zen meditators showed that experienced meditators go into theta brain wave activity. Studies on meditation are now extensive, as outlined by Michael Murphy (1999) in *The Physical and Psychological Effects of Meditation: A Review of Contemporary Research with a Comprehensive Bibliography, 1931–1996*.

Due to the growing interest in meditation and the accumulating evidence that it's so good for us, research has proliferated in recent years. Let's review what researchers are finding. In 2004 scientist Richard Davidson and colleagues reported on EEG studies of monks (Lutz et al. 2004). They found that electrical activity was heightened during meditation in the left *prefrontal cortex*, just behind the forehead. Increased activity in this area is associated with positive emotions. In 2007 Davidson and colleagues reported on studies showing that long-term meditators have more electrical signals in the brain associated with concentration and emotional control (Brefczynski-Lewis et al. 2007). This shows that a practice of meditation leads to having more positive emotions, and the ability to concentrate and regulate emotions.

Sara Lazar is a neuroscientist who investigates how meditation affects our brains. In 2005 she and her colleagues reported the findings of a study where they compared the brains of Western-style mindfulness meditators to those of nonmeditators. They found that an ongoing meditation practice can promote healthy cortical changes in adult brains in areas important for cognitive and emotional processing and well-being. Lazar believes that other forms of yoga and meditation would have a similar positive impact on brain structure.

In other words, meditation is healthy for your brain. Meditation can help reverse the toll that stress takes on your brain by improving concentration, helping you respond in healthier ways to stressful situations or worry, calming you, and boosting your sense of well-being.

breath and healing

The most obvious and immediate way to feel less anxious is by changing how you breathe. Because breathing consciously is so effective, we're introducing it here, in the first chapter, so you can calm your nerves and soothe your body when you need to. We know personally that we don't have to suffer needlessly when just a few deep breaths can restore our well-being. We rely on these breathing practices to support our happiness. Not a day goes by that we don't take deep breaths in the same way we'll teach you to do.

You can literally reverse your body's stress response by changing how you breathe. When you're anxious, focus on taking slow, deep breaths to trigger the relaxation response. Here's why breathing has this effect: Breath is the only physiological function that's controlled by both the voluntary and involuntary nervous systems. Just as with the beating of your heart, the movement of your breath is regulated by the *autonomic*, or involuntary, *nervous system*. You don't have to consciously say, "Breathe in, breathe out." But because breath is also controlled by the voluntary nervous system, you can breathe intentionally. You can lengthen and deepen your breaths. Breathing consciously is at the heart of yoga practices and is a lifesaver that stabilizes you when you're stressed.

PRACTICE: BREATHING INTENTIONALLY

It's easy to experience how breathing intentionally works right now, as you sit there reading this book.

1. Breathe in through your nose and blow the air out through your mouth, as if you were blowing out a candle.

2. Now breathe naturally, in and out through your nose.

3. Repeat this process. Breathe in through your nose, and blow the air out through your mouth, as if you were blowing out a candle.

4. Now breathe naturally, in and out through your nose.

5. Continue breathing normally.

You just altered your breathing. Most likely your breath is now a little deeper, a little more optimal. We do want to note here that in a truly relaxed and "present" state, you don't voluntarily focus on deep breathing; that is, you don't think about or control your breath. However, when you're distressed, you can restore relaxed breathing with this breathing practice.

Deep breathing is optimal and is how you breathe when you're really relaxed. You've probably noticed how full and slow breath is when someone's in deep sleep. Napping babies illustrate this wonderfully. Lying on their backs, babies have innocent bodies that are fully relaxed, and soft bellies that rise and fall with the breath. Unless you've been trained in breathing practices, you probably don't breathe optimally much of the time. If you're among the fortunate few who do, you're probably a calm, clear-thinking person.

The Breath of Anxiety

Even though breathing is governed by the autonomic nervous system, it's influenced by the voluntary nervous system. Chronic anxiety and tension powerfully condition the breath, so much so that sometimes, even when we sleep, our breath doesn't return to optimal breathing.

When you're startled, you gasp and hold your breath, which triggers your body's stress response so that your heart beats faster and your breathing rate increases. When you're chronically anxious, your breath remains rapid and shallow, at least to some degree. Shallow, rapid breathing and anxiety engage in a closed-feedback loop of communication; that is, your anxiety triggers shallow breathing, and your shallow breathing triggers anxiety.

The breath of anxiety is a form of *hyperventilation*—which is faster or deeper breathing, or both—that causes a decrease of carbon dioxide in your blood. It can cause light-headedness, numbness or tingling in the hands or feet, dizziness, chest pain, and slurred speech. If you have a panic attack, hyperventilation is more severe, and if you suffer from chronic anxiety, your breathing is probably a mild form of chronic hyperventilation.

When our breathing is relaxed and we're healthy, our breathing has a natural movement back and forth from breathing primarily through one nostril to the other. If you're healthy, you alternate from right- to left-nostril dominance approximately every two to three hours. The autonomic nervous system, possibly directed by the hypothalamus, is responsible for rotating the breath from one nostril to the other. Anxiety alters this natural rhythm and causes prolonged right-nostril breathing. This interesting fact highlights the delicate interplay of our moods, breathing, and physical body.

Breathe and Become Calm

You can restore diaphragmatic, or optimal, breathing by doing the following practice. Before you begin, we have a tip: Pay more attention to your exhalations than inhalations, because the inbreath that follows a full outbreath is automatically deeper. It takes only a few corrective breaths to restore optimal breathing.

PRACTICE: BREATHING SLOWLY

Sit comfortably and focus on your breathing. You have two alternatives at this point: breathe through pursed lips, as if you were whistling, or gently close off your right nostril with your thumb and breathe through your left nostril. Notice that you can't move as much air. The inability to move as much air begins to ease hyperventilation.

1. Slow down your breathing by breathing in to the count of four and out to the count of six for three full breaths. Don't force the breath. Allow the breath to slowly become fuller.

2. Now resume normal breathing.

After your breathing is more normal, practice belly breathing for a few minutes. This will calm you by activating the parasympathetic relaxation response.

PRACTICE: BELLY BREATHING

Sit comfortably or lie on the floor with your knees bent and your feet on the floor. Lying on the floor is usually more comfortable.

1. Place one hand on your belly just below your ribs. Place the other hand on your chest.

2. Pat your belly, and then pat your chest. You'll find this soothing.

3. Breathe in through your nose.

4. Exhale through pursed lips and feel the hand on your belly fall in toward your spine.

5. Breathe in through your nose and let your belly push your hand out away from your spine.

6. Focus on slow, relaxed exhalations.

7. Repeat these steps three to six times. Take your time and enjoy breathing.

conclusion

Anxiety is very prevalent and has been studied extensively. It involves the body's stress response, and healing from anxiety involves activating the relaxation response. Anxiety lives in your body and mind, and can take many forms. Because your experience of anxiety is unique to you, it helps to get to know exactly how it manifests in your life. Knowing what anxiety does to you helps you recognize it so that you can then develop effective practices for healing from it.

Science has not only discovered the stress response and the relaxation response but has also verified how to restore a healthy balance between tension and relaxation. Whether anxiety stems from thinking or from past trauma, both body and mind are affected, and healing requires calming the body and quieting the mind. Yoga and meditation have been proven to be invaluable in doing both.

In chapter 2 we'll explore causes of anxiety to further your understanding of how and why anxiety lives in you.

chapter 2

how thinking makes you anxious

The fruit of great damage in early childhood, shame causes us to identify with our limitations in such a way that we don't recognize our basic goodness or the possibilities we have to manifest the creative potential of the human spirit.

—Father Thomas Keating

One way or another, thinking winds up being revealed as one of the root causes of our anxiety. Although we're aware that thinking is in the mix, how it relates to anxiety can seem a little mysterious. One reason it's baffling is that we're often unaware of the thoughts that play a major role in anxiety. They work on us beneath our level of awareness. The kinds of thoughts that fuel anxiety are those that tell us we're not worthy, that we're flawed human beings. These painful thoughts, which don't have a clue about our basic goodness, smolder and ignite into anxiety, and have usually been with us since childhood.

Another way thinking contributes is by escalating the resulting anxiety when we're triggered into a flashback. For example, a veteran may have the fight-or-flight response of past combat experience when there's a loud bang, such as when an object has been dropped on the floor nearby. When this occurs, no apparent thoughts have created the anxiety, nor is there an actual external threat. Still, in the split second after the startle, the veteran's mind naturally reacts with thoughts like, *What! Oh, my God, what!* which feed the fear. Additionally, talking about or remembering the old trauma can trigger a flashback. No matter what the original cause, even if it's biological or environmental, your mind reacts to feeling anxious in a way that tends to perpetuate and increase your anxiety, for example, when you think, *Oh, no, here it comes again!* after starting to feel those familiar nervous feelings.

thinking plays a major role in anxiety

Let's look at where the thoughts that cause anxiety come from. Often, they're automatic and familiar, so much so that you're oblivious to them, consider them to be normal, or both. These are thoughts about who you believe you are. If, as the fruit of childhood wounding, you believe that you're an inferior person, you have a deep belief that becomes a self-fulfilling prophecy. You carry it around in your head throughout your life and suffer from the pain associated with it. Believing a lie like that, one that says you're less than others, is a root cause of anxiety.

Inferiority Complex

You've heard of the term *inferiority complex*, which refers to a strong underlying feeling of personal inferiority that frequently causes either inhibited or aggressive behavior, the latter in over-compensation for the feelings of inferiority. Believing that you're not capable enough creates a lack of trust in your ability to navigate through life. You may avoid risk taking, and seek to play it safe in order to avoid provoking your anxiety. It's a little like being afraid of your own shadow and therefore avoiding going out in the sun. As a result, you may not feel anxious, but your world becomes small, confined, and stagnant. If you believe that you're unlovable, you may feel nervous from wondering if you'll be left behind, feel that others are slighting you, or fear mistreatment by those you live with.

Alternatively, you may have responded to a sense of being inferior by overcompensating for it. Many people pick themselves up by their own bootstraps. Through hard work and pure grit, they make themselves "good enough." If this describes you, your efforts probably helped you along in your life. However, you may have a gnawing feeling that you're an imposter, and fear that others will find out that you're not as smart as you'd like them to think you are. You probably try hard and strive toward perfection. Rather than trust your instincts and intelligence, you defer to standards you've adopted. Then, as the years go by, it may dawn on you that you don't know yourself. That's when you may discover the deep currents of anxiety that have lived in you for a long time.

If any or all of these descriptions fit you, read on so you can, at last, discover who you are beneath your sense of inferiority.

identifying with thoughts

Thoughts are as intimate as your breath in that they live inside you and can affect every aspect of life. Thoughts are so close yet can't be seen and, generally, live beneath the radar screen of your awareness. You have many more thoughts than you realize. As a result the dramatic impact that thoughts have on your life is usually obscure. It's as if you have a secret life in your thinking mind that projects out into your conscious world.

Many of the thoughts that cause anxiety have their origins in childhood. They're as familiar in your inner landscape as the motion of your breathing. They reside in the background of your awareness like the rumbling sound of distant thunder. While thoughts may seem as harmless as distant thunder, they're not. Unconscious thoughts exert great influence. Thoughts can have a great impact, whether they're perceived or unconscious. Therefore, it's important to understand your relationship with your thoughts.

You're More than Your Thoughts

Essential to your ability to reduce your anxiety is realizing that you're much more than what you think. You can't be totally described, confined, or contained by the words you think or speak. This is very good news because it means that no concept or idea comes close to capturing the essence of who you are. Realizing that words don't define you is a huge insight, one that helps you to stop believing words that cause you to feel bad about who you are.

Self-referential thoughts are words that you think or say to describe yourself. Whether they build you up or tear you down, such thoughts are, at best, inaccurate and only a partial expression of who you are. The thoughts you hear may range from *Something's wrong with me* to *I'm special.* Whatever the content of your thoughts, they're an incomplete definition or description of who you are. You can make a long list of everything you think describes you, but you'll never be able to make a totally sufficient list. The content of your thoughts doesn't define you, because the thinking mind is only one aspect of who you are. Not only that, but the thinking mind is inherently limited in its ability to grasp the totality of who you are.

Even though you're immensely more than your thoughts, you unavoidably identity with them. As a result, when you say, "I am afraid," you momentarily identify with fear. The words "I am afraid" have a linking, bonding element to them. You identify yourself with what comes after the "I am," for example, "I am funny," "I am a genius," "I am sad," "I am terribly upset," "I am creative," "I am not creative," and so on. It's as if the words after "I am" are your name, which you relate to as if it's all that you are in the moment it's spoken.

Adopting a Story of Identity

The sense of becoming a "somebody," an "I am," occurs quite early in childhood. Call a four-year-old by the wrong name, and she'll likely tell you who she is: "I'm not Suzie; I'm Sue!" Identifying with your given name is an obvious example of using words to characterize who you are.

While it's human nature to identity with thoughts as you develop, there's more to it. Humans are storytellers. Even as a child, you told stories to yourself about who you are. Like every story, stories of self-identity have themes. Stories about who you are circulate around two core themes, personal competency and lovability. The theme of competency shows up as variations of "I'm smart," "I'm a slow learner," "I'm a success," "I'm a failure," "Things come easily for me," and "Life's hard for me." The list is never ending. The theme of lovability shows up as variations of "I'm loved," "I have to earn love," "Nobody's there for me," "I have a big heart," "I have to take care of others in order to be loved," and "I'm not okay as I am."

Your story of who you are is based on comparisons to others. In fact, it's essential to have a reference point for comparison. Your mind assesses your story of identity by how you feel your personal qualities compare or contrast to those of others: "I'm smarter than my brother," "I'm quieter than the other kids," "I'm more popular than most," or "I'm the favored child of my mother."

Stories of identity are based on your individualized experiences of circumstances and relationships that occurred during childhood. These stories live on in your psyche until and unless you see them for what they are: stories that you hold onto in your mind. This means that unless you become aware of the stories, complete with themes, attitudes, and beliefs about who you are, you unconsciously live them out in life. Much anxiety stems from these self-limiting stories that you created in childhood, especially those stories that you formed around trauma and adversity.

Why Your Story Matters

To evolve and to overcome anxiety, it's essential that your old stories about who you thought you were become transparent to you. When you become conscious of old stories, they begin to lose their energetic grip on your life. Then, when you realize that some old story is affecting your life, you can respond with, "Wow, it's that old story again." When you see a big pothole in the road, you can slow down or drive around it. In the same manner, when you become aware of your old story, it doesn't have the same impact on or control over your life. If you don't see your story, you get stuck in it over and over again. Note that we're not recommending that you avoid your story; we're suggesting that you get to know it and understand how it affects you so that it doesn't keep you trapped in the same old anxiety-producing ruts.

Unfortunately, millions of people believe stories of identity that drag them down. If your story diminishes you in any way, it can drive you into some painful and stressful places. For example, if your story is about being unlovable, you may find yourself in relationships where you're not nurtured, or in a lifestyle or career that's not personally fulfilling. Reliving "I'm not good enough" stories can erode your health and create much anxiety and suffering.

The results of a major study of over 17,400 middle-income individuals conducted at Kaiser Permanente HMO in San Diego verified that adverse childhood experiences occur much more frequently than is generally acknowledged. In the study, reported by Dr. V. J. Felitti and colleagues (1998), 50 percent of the respondents reported having lived through adversity in early life. Adverse childhood experiences were categorized as follows: childhood emotional, physical, and sexual abuse; emotional or physical neglect; witnessing domestic violence, or parental separation or divorce; and growing up with drug-abusing, mentally ill, suicidal, or criminal household members. It's noteworthy that half of the middle-income respondents reported having seen or gone through painful experiences as children. This study makes it obvious that trauma and difficulties are pervasive and cross all socioeconomic lines. The impact of adverse childhood experiences was also covered in the study. Not surprisingly, the greater the number of adverse situations encountered in childhood, the more significant the effect. The effects ranged from anxiety, depression, and alcoholism to physical health problems and even premature death.

Before continuing, we want to add some perspective. People respond differently to adversity, and early life circumstances don't automatically determine your fate. Your childhood experiences themselves don't necessarily determine the story you tell yourself about yourself. At least there's not a one-to-one relationship between the two. Millions of people come from horrible childhoods, but they put their stories together in different ways. For example, three brothers can grow up in pretty much the same violent and abusive family but come out with very different stories because of their individualized ways of putting their experiences together in their minds. Even more powerful than what happens to you are the stories you believe about what happened.

We've discussed how trauma lives on in the body. Here we're stressing that stories live on as well. If you underestimate the influence of your early childhood on your current life, disregarding the power of old beliefs, you may relive anxiety for years to come and not live fully. To break the cycle of anxiety, it's essential to look deeply into the nature of the old core stories that cause anxiety.

PRACTICE: WHAT'S YOUR STORY OF IDENTITY?

1. Ask yourself, "What kind of person am I?"

2. Listen for the answers that come from within you. What story themes do you hear?

3. Ask yourself, "Do I believe I'm competent? Do I believe I'm lovable?"

4. Write your answers in a journal or notebook.

Conditioned Self-Identity

The stories that you believe describe you are called the *conditioned self-identity*. You absorbed these ideas from the environment around you, and as such, they're external to you in that what you heard didn't originate in you. For example, if a young child is consistently told that she's not as smart as her brother, she naturally factors her interpretation of that statement into her story about how smart she is. We know many bright people who believe they aren't smart enough; you probably do as well. Yet, in all reality, none of us can be reduced to what our parents said or didn't say about us. In the same manner, you can't be defined by what did and didn't happen to you. While you were powerfully impacted by childhood events in that whatever you experienced lives on because it became a part of the story of you, what happened back then doesn't come close to describing the full truth of who you are.

You may think you've left the past behind, and in some respects you have. But unless you've thoroughly examined your stories, your ways of dealing with emotions, your interpersonal patterns, your strategies for success and failure, and your strategies for getting or rejecting love, you unwittingly perpetuate the stories that arose out of your early life. Unless there's a significant shift of consciousness, your sense of identity stems from how you were raised.

PRACTICE: EXPLORE YOUR STORY OF IDENTITY

Learn more about your story of identity by completing the following sentences:

- I'm the kind of person who _____.

- I've always believed that I was _____.

- I describe myself as _____.

self-worth

Unfortunately, many of us believe that we have to earn or build self-worth, not knowing that we're inherently valuable beyond measure. Many parents don't realize how precious their children are, not because they're unloving or unskilled parents but because they don't know that all human life is precious. Deep inside, they don't feel that their own lives are sacred. Only when parents know that they themselves are utterly precious "just because," can they fully transmit that message to their children. If they didn't receive that message from their parents or discover it on their own, they have no recourse but to believe their interpretation of their conditioning and unknowingly pass on to their children what was passed down to them. What gets passed on, generation after generation, is a misunderstanding about self-worth, that it's conditional rather than unconditional.

Consciously or unconsciously, we have a burning desire to know and experience ourselves as whole and worthy. This yearning may motivate you, as it does countless others. Not knowing that you're already whole may cause you to react by adopting some story about what a good person is like and then modeling your life according to how you think you should be. You compensate for not knowing your sacred worth by making yourself into what you think you should be.

Betty's Story of Identity

> I was raised in rural New York by my divorced mother, who was mentally ill. My mom was afraid of water and forbade us to go near lakes. To this day, I'm terrified of deep water. It's my secret; even my husband of thirty years and two daughters don't know. I'm so ashamed; being unable to swim shows my poverty. I don't want people to know that I was raised as a poor girl. I went to college and married well, and I've worked hard to improve myself. I don't want anyone to know that I can't swim, so I make up convincing lies to avoid the water.

Betty unavoidably believed that who she was reflected her upbringing, as we all do. Having little sense of being a valuable, precious human being, she was identified with being painfully poor, as if that were who she was. The facet of anxiety she manifested was "Something's wrong with me." Even though she's well educated and wealthy, she identifies with a core story of being less than others. She experienced three adverse childhood experiences: parental divorce, her mother's mental illness, and emotional abuse. Betty compensated for her resultant flawed sense of self by becoming a self-made woman. She graduated from college with honors, maintains an impeccable appearance, and tries to be a great friend. However, she suffers from chronic anxiety and panic attacks, not just because she fears that someone will find out about her childhood but because, in spite of her valiant efforts to make herself into a good-enough person, she unconsciously believes, as she did as an innocent young girl, that she's not as worthy as others.

Primary Perspectives

Betty, like you and everyone else, grew up and perpetuated her conditioned self and its stories by seeing self, others, and the world through the primary perspectives contained in her core story. Her story was "Because I was raised poor, I'm not as good as others." The primary perspectives become filtered lenses that you see out of. Because these lenses are distorted perceptions, you don't see yourself and others as they are. The perspective "Something's wrong with me" is pervasive and expressed in phrases such as "I'm not like others," "Why can't I be like him?" "I could never do that," and "It never works for me." These perspectives color your world negatively and contribute mightily to anxiety.

"Something's Wrong with Me" and the Fear of Public Speaking

When, deep within, you think you're not okay, tension results, which may cause you to rely on reassurance from others that you're okay and prompt you to interpret looks from others as critical. This painful mix of needing approval and seeing disapproval causes you to hold back, for fear of doing it wrong, and is a root cause of social anxiety, the most prevalent anxiety disorder in the United States, according to R. C. Kessler and colleagues (2005), who reported that 15 million American adults aged eighteen and older, or about 6.8 percent of people in this age group, have social phobia. Fear of public speaking is fueled by the fear that the audience will judge you negatively or that you'll make a fool of yourself. You worry that your inadequacy will be exposed and that speaking to a group will be humiliating. Fear of public speaking demonstrates that you not only see outwardly through your primary perspectives but also inwardly. The lenses distort vision both ways. If you perceive others as judging you, you also judge yourself. If you magnify your faults, you see others as magnifying your faults.

If you find the thought of public speaking terrifying, you're not doomed. You can examine the core stories that fuel this fear. As you're about to discover, you don't have to look at life through the same old perceptual lenses.

Innocent Misunderstanding

What follows are two really empowering practices that enabled us to speak in front of groups, and they can help you as well. To review, anxiety about public speaking is spurred on by a gross misunderstanding that comes out of your story about yourself. You literally believe something untrue that causes you anxiety. You can clear up the misperception by taking two healing steps. The first step is to identify your old story of identity. The second step is to call it by its true name: "innocent misunderstanding."

PRACTICE: CONTINUE EXPLORING YOUR STORY OF IDENTITY

What's your old story of the kind of person you are? Get to know it well so that it no longer affects you unconsciously. To continue your investigation, here are five more sentences to complete:

- The biggest lie I've believed about who I am is _____.

- What I don't want others to know about who I am is _____.

- Deep inside, I always thought I was _____.

- My parents thought I was _____.

- Summing it up, a phrase that best describes the kind of person I am is _____.

PRACTICE: INNOCENT MISUNDERSTANDING

1. Read what you wrote in the previous practice.

2. After each sentence, pause, breathe deeply, and say out loud, "Old, old story, such an innocent misunderstanding."

You may say "such an innocent misunderstanding" endless times. Say it whenever you hear the old core story or feel it manifesting in your life. Each time you do this, you bring more healing. You heal because you speak the truth. Your conditioned identity is the innocent misunderstanding of a child.

conclusion

Your old story of who you are has great influence over you. It lives on in your subconscious mind, beneath your awareness, as a cause and perpetuator of your anxiety. But you're not destined to live out your days believing old stories and reliving past adversity. The healing practices of yoga help you see how your mind functions, give you great comfort, and connect you with your inner essence.

chapter 3

how yoga heals anxiety

This act of witness is pure. It does not strive to be kind; it is
just a good companion. And out of this companionship arises
compassion…. We accompany our own pains and thoughts
and hopes, whatever arises in the mind and heart—and notice
kindly, as if what arises were a child, a lover, our oldest friend.

—John Tarrant

as soon as you start looking into the old stories that contribute to anxiety, you're on your way to healing. It doesn't take much looking for you to appreciate how much suffering those innocent misunderstandings cause. Just knowing about them is a relief, and motivates you to continue looking inside. You realize how unaware you were of the source of your pain, and you understand in a very personal way what Socrates meant when he said, "An unexamined life is not worth living."

becoming conscious

To support your inward gazing, we'll discuss what happens when we look inside ourselves. To summarize John Tarrant's comments in the chapter-opening epigraph, witnessing is a way to be in relationship with ourselves. You become the one who's observing as well as the one who's experiencing. When you watch a great dancer onstage, you're in relationship with someone else. When you notice your frantic dance of rushing hither and yon, you're in relationship with yourself. While you're truly watching someone else, you forget yourself, and while you're truly watching yourself, you find yourself. It may even prompt you to say, "Here I am, hurrying around." Then an interesting thing is likely to happen. You may find yourself slowing down. Simply becoming aware relieves you. Witnessing is how you become aware.

The Practice of Witnessing

Witnessing is the ability to observe thoughts, emotions, physical sensations, and energy—all the activity that goes on inside you. Witnessing is paying attention to yourself as you do when you're aware of your surroundings. You learned to observe traffic when you drive, watch over your children at play, or keep an eye on the stove when you're cooking a meal. Although you learned how to focus your attention, your ability to observe is an innate capacity. You can also learn how to pay attention to what's happening in your inner world. You cultivate this capacity through practice.

PRACTICE: SIMPLE WITNESSING

1. Look around where you are right now. Notice the colors and shapes. Examine something closely, noticing its colors, shapes, or textures.

2. Now put your attention on yourself. Rub two fingers together and feel what that's like. Pause and breathe. Note the sensation of your buttocks on your chair. Pause and breathe. Now perceive the sensation of your heart's beating.

3. Put your attention on your environment again. Look at the colors, shapes, and textures that surround you.

4. Move your attention inside again. Notice the sensations of the bottoms of your feet on the floor.

5. Gaze at your hands and notice the sensation of energy pulsing through them.

Notice how enjoyable this practice is! Your mind becomes absorbed in witnessing and finds it pleasurable. Notice that there's no judgment in witnessing; it's pure noticing. It's one thing to notice but far more healing to notice that you're noticing. In this practice you were conscious that you were witnessing.

The Practice of Conscious Breathing

When your breathing relaxes, so does your body. One way to slow your breath is to intentionally breathe deeply, as we discussed in chapter 1. Doing so triggers the relaxation response, and is big medicine for anxiety. When you breathe consciously, your breath becomes an anchor that prevents you from being carried away by anxiety.

Another way to relax your breath is to pay attention to it. Simply noticing your breath without intending to deepen it can be soothing, because when you witness your breath, you don't pay attention to your thinking. Your attention is occupied with breathing, and your mind becomes quiet. Therefore, a powerful practice is simply placing your awareness on your breath: *breath coming in, breath going out, breath coming in, and breath going out.* If you're a hurrier, you may have skipped over the last sentence. If you did, it's okay; just notice that you did. Anxious minds do tend to rush. Try it again: *breath coming in, breath going out.* When you actually slow down and practice, you feel calmer.

The Practice of Inquiry

When you feel anxious, most of your attention is occupied with racing thoughts and fearful feelings. Those intense sensations are your primary state, what you most identify with. Internally you don't just feel that you're *experiencing* anxiety, you feel that you *are* anxiety.

However, when you inquire into anxiety, it becomes more of a secondary state, or at least a shared primary state. You no longer experience yourself solely as anxiety. You become a person who's experiencing anxiety but who is also inquiring. Identify with being an investigator of your experience, and curiosity becomes your primary state. You, as an interested person, are studying anxiety. This different point of view helps you to avoid getting lost in anxiety. More than an anxious person, you're now a person *having* anxiety and *learning* about it.

The practice of inquiry helps make you aware that you're more than what you experience. You, a conscious being, have experiences and can learn what causes these experiences. Inquiry helps you understand your internal world of sensations, emotions, motives, and perceptions. It also helps you get to the bottom of how you perpetuate anxiety. A great way to look beneath your surface experiences, inquiry is an investigation into how your mind functions, how your beliefs impact you, and how your past experiences regenerate themselves.

Reading this book helps you inquire into anxiety so you can question it and not take your ordinary experience for granted. You already did an inquiry when you looked into your story of identity and completed the sentences about your beliefs about yourself. There are many more sentence-completion practices in the book. We encourage you to be curious as you work through these practices, clearing out old false misunderstandings and uncovering the truth about who you really are.

The Practice of Practicing

We humans are creatures of habit. Habits such as anxiety become automatic and deeply entrenched through repetition. While we form many of our habits unintentionally or unconsciously, we can also develop habits intentionally. Yoga practices will help you cultivate new habits, like how to deal with anxiety rather than be controlled by it. The cumulative effect of a wisely selected regular yoga practice is that you enjoy life more and can take new risks, and if you're anxious, at least it isn't debilitating.

Mary's Story

As we said, Mary suffered from anxiety for many years. After attending yoga classes for a couple of years, the deeper practices of breath awareness, witnessing, and heart meditations took root and began releasing anxiety's grip on her. This story tells how repeated practice relieves anxiety:

A few years ago, I began teaching seminars and traveling around the country. Traveling alone wasn't easy for me. I'm directionally impaired and get turned around easily. I don't like being lost, and I become terrified. My mind becomes irrational, believing that I'll be lost forever. Thanks to yoga practices, I now recognize my distress when I'm driving in unfamiliar places, breathe deeply to remain in the present moment, do a reality check on my worrisome thoughts, and find my way. I travel around the country alone, not always comfortably, but fear doesn't stop me.

On one trip, I decided to follow complex directions and make my way in my rental car across the city to a restaurant. While driving, my familiar scary thoughts popped up: What if I can't find my way back to the hotel? This is too hard. This is confusing. I should never have left the hotel. *My autonomic nervous system revved up and I felt anxious. At the same time, I witnessed my thoughts and focused on taking full breaths:* breathe in, breathe out; breathe in, breathe out. *Reasoning returned and I could do a reality check:* Look, you're not lost. You have the GPS and a cell phone. It's daylight. *I practiced comforting self-talk:* It's okay, you're okay.

I made it to the restaurant and asked for a table in a quiet area. Once seated, I began the soothing yoga practice of putting my hand on my heart. I breathed fully, sensed into my heart, and felt the warmth of compassion. Feeling supported, I saw, in a fresh and deep way, how entrenched those old fearful thoughts were. Deep grooves in the unconscious, they've been there for a long time.

I wept unseen tears, realizing once again how pervasively fearful thoughts have plagued me. I felt loving-kindness toward this conditioned personality. Miraculously, since then,

fear hasn't overwhelmed me when I've been in unfamiliar
cities. However, if it arises again, I know I have the support of
breath awareness, loving-kindness, and the sanity that comes
from witnessing thoughts and emotions.

The healing practices of yoga can transform your relationship to anxiety, just as they've done and continue to do for Mary.
Develop the practice of practicing. Then, when anxiety grips you,
these practices are embedded in you, ready to serve.

the five capacities of the mind

You can't deal with what you're unaware of. One of the great benefits
of the practice of witnessing is that you become conscious of your
mental activity. So that you can actually do so, it's helpful to know
what you're looking at. This section gives you some pointers.

Perhaps when you were a child, someone pointed out to you
the star constellations in the night sky. Standing beside you, maybe
someone raised a hand and pointed out the Big Dipper and the
Milky Way. Then, because you knew what to look for, you saw
them for the first time. As soon as you could recognize them, the
experience of looking at the stars became one of delight. So that
you know what to look for, yoga has outlined the five capacities of
the mind, making it possible for you to look into your mind and
call your thoughts by their true names. Doing so is as gratifying as
naming star constellations in the night sky, because what was once
obscure now becomes apparent.

According to the yoga tradition, the functioning of the adult
mind is divided into five capacities:

- Memory

- Imagination

- Perception

- Sense of identity

- Intelligence

Memory

One of the functions of your mind is to store and remember information. Memory allows you to recall where you live, where you work, which bank account is yours, and your preferred foods. While memory is important for healthy living, being preoccupied in the memory takes you away from the present moment and orients your current life to events in the past.

Feeling the tug of the past is easy to experience. Here's a memory about kindness:

I remember my sweet German shepherd. Many years ago, one particularly emotional day, I sat in my recliner, crying. My beloved eighty-five-pound dog crawled up on my lap and began licking my tears and whimpering. Touched by her compassion, I hugged her and my tears subsided. Writing now, I feel the emotional tug of the memory. She was a wonderful companion for me.

If you like, try it yourself. Pull up a memory of kindness. Feel its effect on you. Notice how it pulls at you and, for an instant, you disconnect from the present and go back in time. Dwell for a while in that experience, and then come back to the present moment.

Imagination

The human mind also has the function of imagination. A wonderful capacity, it's the means by which great music, art, innovation, and humor emerge. Yet your imagination can scare you by focusing on what *might be*. When you're preoccupied with the future, you're living through your imagination. You're absorbed in what might happen and aren't paying attention to the present moment. Being oriented toward the future is a hallmark characteristic of anxiety. It doesn't matter whether the future is the next moment, day, or week, or years from now.

Living in the future is also easy to experience. Here's an example:

I'm looking forward to a desired event, a reunion with a couple of sweet nieces. We haven't seen each other for over a year. They're very dear to me, and I'm eager to hug them and spend time with them. Writing now, I'm smiling in anticipation, because I love them so!

Try it yourself. Anticipate some desired event that you're looking forward to. Feel its effect on you. Notice how it pulls at you and, for an instant, you disconnect from the present and move into the imagined future. Now, come back to the present moment!

Perception

One of the functions of your mind is perception, which is how you take in data from outside your body. You use your senses to take in information from the physical world around you. Have a direct experience of how you take in information:

1. Pause for a moment and look at a color in your immediate environment.

2. Now listen to the sounds around you.

3. Taste any lingering flavor in your mouth.

4. Smell scents on your clothes and hands.

5. Touch and feel this book.

Perceptions are frequently distorted because we interpret the raw information coming in through our senses through the filters of our beliefs and survival instincts. Inevitably, the thoughts that underlie anxiety distort perception. Here's an obvious example: If you believe you're unattractive, then you're likely to think that others see you as unsightly. When someone turns and looks at you, you assume they're judging you negatively. Your eyes take in data, and then the data goes through the filters of the conditioned mind. Your anxiety is caused by how you interpret being looked at, not the fact that someone sees you.

Sense of Identity

Another function of the mind is to develop an identity, a sense of "who I am." This enables you to experience yourself as a distinct individual. Gradually, your sense of who you are becomes ingrained and unquestioned.

Even your name isn't who you are in your essence. It was given to you. Your name is a word associated with you that says nothing about who you really are. Of course, much more than your name goes into your sense of identity. The point here is that even your given name is an aspect of your conditioning.

At the surface level, you may find that your self-identity has changed and become more positive. But in reality, the old story remains untouched by your efforts to make yourself worthy. Improving your assessment of yourself through good deeds and positive words is like painting over old wood. Painting protects the surface and looks good, but underneath, the wood remains unchanged. Although it may make you feel better to paint over the old story, the most profound healing comes from recognizing that your story isn't who you are anyway.

It's not wrong to develop a story of who you are; it's a natural function of your mind. However, it's just one aspect of your mind, not the totality of who you are. When you understand this, you begin to free yourself from the grip of your stories. Once you learn to recognize your core stories, they don't have the same old magnetic pull on you, even though you may occasionally get sucked in for a while. We still do, and then, sooner or later, it dawns on us that we're caught up in the undertow of our old stories. Once we become aware, we see our stories for what they are, innocent misunderstandings, rather than believe they're who we are.

Intelligence

The mind has another function: intelligence. In the West we typically think of intelligence, or IQ, as a grouping of capacities that can be measured by objective testing. The form of intelligence we refer to here is better understood as wisdom, and could also be called insight, clarity, and knowing. You can't force wisdom or inner knowing. It simply arises or pops up, often when your mind is quiet. For example, you probably sometimes wrestle with a problem in the evening when you're exhausted. In your fatigue you can't decide what to do. Finally, you give up and say something to yourself like, "Good grief, this is getting you nowhere. Just go to bed." The next morning, the solution to the problem dawns on you and seems obvious.

Letting your thinking mind take a break from your problems makes such good sense. You already know you don't make your best decisions when you worry and fret, which generally amounts to thinking the same thoughts over and over. Find ways to quiet your mind with the meditation practices outlined in chapter 7, and the answers you access will be far more intelligent than the ones that worrisome thoughts generate.

Become Aware of How the Mind Functions

When you go on a long car trip, a map helps you identify where you are. Yoga helps you recognize where you are in your mind by teaching you how the mind functions and how to witness it. You can become aware of your mind's inner workings. With practice you can witness having a memory, imagining the future, or repeating the same old story of identity. And, as you experienced in the witnessing practice earlier in the chapter, witnessing is relational. You, the witness, become a companion to you, the thinker and experiencer.

This is truly encouraging. When you can see what your mind is doing, you don't totally identify with your thoughts. You aren't as consumed by them, so you don't drive yourself as crazy. Being driven by subconscious thoughts is like driving at night with your headlights off. You can't see where you're going. On the other hand, with your witnessing lights on, you can see what's going on inside your mind that causes anxiety, and you no longer blindly continue down the same painful road.

Cynthia's Story

During a recent conversation, Cynthia said, "I'm very anxious, and I doubt my decision to spend the summer in India. I can't sleep and I question my motivation for going." When asked about her original motive for the upcoming journey, she responded, "I've felt pulled toward this spiritual community for many years. I want to go to see if I can participate and contribute."

When asked how long she had experienced doubt when making significant life decisions, she responded, "Doubt has been with me for as long as I remember." When asked if doubt gave her insight, she hesitated and whispered, "Doubt simply doubts. That's all it does; it doesn't guide me. It makes me insecure." She was quiet for a moment, and then added, "Listening to doubt has caused me great anxiety. Doubt questions my motives, makes me distrust myself." She sat in silence, soaking in the impact of her words, and added, "Doubt causes pain. Doubt can only doubt." A yoga practitioner, Cynthia focused on her breathing, giving herself time to digest what she had said. She inquired into doubt and realized that it was her imagination scaring her with "what if's." She named it "the 'Double Doubter,' who hesitates and questions my motives, causing me to distrust what I know in my heart is true."

Seeing that her imagination had scared her, and breathing through the emotional discomfort enabled her to reconnect with her genuine longing to spend time in this spiritual community. She didn't need to analyze a lifetime of doubt. Seeing doubt for what it was, she stepped outside it, into the inner space of breath, witnessing, and the capacity to think clearly.

embracing consciousness as healer

You probably carry on conversations with yourself, even try to help yourself, by talking back to your worrisome thoughts. Cynthia could have countered her doubting thoughts with reassuring ones: *I don't know if I should take this trip* could have been opposed with *It's okay, you're just having second thoughts.* Substituting a more nurturing thought is often very helpful. However, you can't substitute an encouraging thought if you aren't aware of what you're thinking, and sometimes simply witnessing what's going on is all that's needed.

Cynthia practiced observing how her mind was functioning. She witnessed the worrisome thought, *What if the trip doesn't go well and this is a big mistake?* and noted, *These are doubt thoughts; my imagination is scaring me.* Becoming aware of the thoughts and redirecting awareness back to her breath calmed her and brought her back into the present moment, where she could access intelligence: *Here I am, in this moment, thinking these thoughts! Here's doubt again.*

By focusing on breathing, she disengaged from her thoughts and saw that they only served one function, to scare her. Cynthia felt a burst of energy when she saw her doubt for what it was. Her anxiety transformed into excitement.

Like Cynthia, your healing is a journey of understanding what happens inside you that causes your discomfort. Cynthia looked into her doubt and realized it had been with her for as long as she could remember. Once she became aware of its presence and named it "Double Doubter," she was empowered to follow her heart's desire.

Remember how Mary, who, in spite of being directionally impaired, now travels regularly across the country by herself? For as long as Mary could remember, she had believed the thought, *I'm unable to travel alone.* Other thoughts, such as *I don't learn things easily* and *I'm not really intelligent,* reinforced her sense of inadequacy. The deeper underlying story of identity was, *I'm not competent enough.*

For Mary, recognizing the story of identity was liberating. This story hasn't gone away, because it has deep roots in her psyche. However, the story doesn't have the emotional power that it once did and that was once the source of so much anxiety. Nor does it limit her. When she sees the story, she whispers, "Old, old story, innocent misunderstanding." She watches the activity of her mind and breathes, and expresses gratitude for the freedom from its bondage.

Anxiety causes a shrinking in consciousness and a reduction in your sense of self. Growing in consciousness expands your sense of self; as you learn more about yourself, you discover that there's much more to you than you ever dreamed possible.

PRACTICE: EXPLORE YOUR POTENTIALITY

1. Take time to pause and center your awareness in your body.

2. **Become aware of your body.** Feel your hip bones on your chair and your feet on the floor. Feel your spine rise up out of your pelvis. Relax your shoulders. Relax your jaws.

3. **Become aware of your energy.** Notice your breath come in and out of your nostrils. Now notice breath come into and out of your chest. Now notice that breath moves into and out of your belly. Enjoy your breath!

4. Now, inquire into your potentiality by completing the following sentences:

    •   What I truly want for myself is _____.

    •   My deepest yearning is to _____.

    •   What really matters to me is _____.

    •   If I could, I would _____.

5. In a journal write what you truly want and what touches your heart. Tell your innermost desires to someone you trust.

To support your expansion, we turn to an exploration of who you truly are. Anxiety becomes less significant when you become aware of the significance of who you are.

the five sheaths

In yoga, *sheath* is a term used to describe the different layers of our being. Often compared to the layers of an onion, they span from our more superficial and apparent physical body to the more subtle and deeper "bodies" of the emotions, mind, and spirit. These sheaths familiarize you with your inner landscape and help you identify and map out what you experience and where you experience it. This is most helpful as you become more aware of your thoughts, emotions, and energy that correspond to anxiety and those that correspond to being contented. Next we discuss the five sheaths, beginning with the outermost and ending with the innermost:

- Food sheath

- Energy (or prana) sheath

- Mental sheath

- Subtle (Buddhi, or wisdom) sheath

- Bliss sheath

The Food Sheath

The outermost body is the *food sheath*. Also known as the physical body, it's the flesh and bones that make up the body you dwell in. Although you live in the body, you aren't confined to it. You may identify primarily with your body, even determine self-esteem based on how you judge its relative beauty. However, the tissues that make up your organs, skeleton, and muscles are only one dimension of your being. Tissues are transient and ever changing. The cells that comprise the body continually regenerate.

The Energy, or Prana, Sheath

The *energy body*, or *prana*, is the movement of energy through your physical and mental sheaths. Life doesn't exist without prana; we depend on it to move our physical bodies, pump blood, digest food, breathe, think, and concentrate. We experience energy on a continuum of intensity, from intense to lethargic.

The stress response stirs up prana and creates energy blocks in the body. You know what that's like. Your heart beats quickly; your muscles pulse with energy, ready to take action; and your mind focuses sharply. If there's no need to fight or flee, or there's no immediate release for the pent-up energy, your mind shifts from a singular focus to racing thoughts, and your body becomes jittery or tense. The relaxation response calms your energy. When the parasympathetic nervous system is activated, your mind becomes quiet. Your heart rate slows down, your digestion improves, your physical body feels at ease, and you experience a sense of well-being.

Yoga works with prana primarily through breathing exercises and physical postures. Deepening and slowing the breath settles the prana body. Stretching and moving the body through physical postures releases tension from your muscles.

Mental Sheath

The *mental sheath* consists of the basic functioning of the mind. The mind remembers, imagines, perceives, and forms a sense of identity, as we discussed earlier.

- Memory consists of selective storage of events from the past. It's neither complete nor accurate.

- Imagination is conjecture, fantasy, and play. It anticipates the future, something that doesn't even exist.

- Sense of identity is the story about who you think you are that you have adopted and maintained.

Believing your story of self-worth is as confused as believing that you're the outmost appearance of your body! It simply isn't true.

Yoga practices help you realize that your story of who you are is just a story and that you're inherently good. The truth is, you're intrinsically good. Your healing task is to discover this truth. Then you don't have to add anything extra to feel good. In your core you're not flawed, so there's nothing to fix and nothing to prove.

Subtle Sheath (Buddhi, or Wisdom)

The next innermost sheath, the *subtle sheath*, or *Buddhi*, generally shows up when the mind is quiet. Buddhi is also called the "still, small voice within" or the "voice of inner guidance." Your inner guidance wants what's true for you regardless of your fears, painful memories, or negative self-talk. It doesn't want for you to stay stuck in anxiety, even though your fearful and doubting thoughts may argue against its advice and justify or defend staying where you are. Ignoring inner guidance results in more anxiety. So although you may be afraid, putting off doing what you know, deep inside, you need to do simply prolongs your stress.

Inner guidance comes easier if you don't try to control, lead, or direct it. We may try to lead guidance in order to get specific, predetermined answers, as if we know what's best and are soliciting help to achieve our goals. When we construct or attempt to force guidance, we may end up suppressing it. Asking for inner guidance is a way to seek input from your higher self, or higher power. While it's tempting to tell it what to do, asking for open-ended guidance is a way to open up to true guidance. Questions such as "What do I really need to know right now?" and "What is life calling me to do?" help us access something deeper than the mind's chatter.

PRACTICE: LISTENING TO INNER GUIDANCE

1. **Become aware of your body.** Feel your hip bones on your chair and your feet on the floor. Feel your spine rise up out of your pelvic floor. Relax your shoulders. Relax your jaw.

2. **Become aware of your energy.** Notice your breath move in and out of your nostrils. Notice breath move into and out of your chest. Now notice breath move into and out of your belly.

3. **Ask for guidance.** Place your hand on your heart and breathe into your chest. Ask for nondirected guidance. Sit quietly and listen. Wait. Create an opening for guidance to come through. You may experience a voice, a feeling, or a knowing, or you may experience this process as you would a dream or daydream. Receive whatever you hear with an open mind. Writing it down and speaking it out loud make it more real for you, so write what you hear in a journal or notebook and then tell it to someone you trust.

Bliss Sheath

The innermost body, the *bliss sheath* is the essence of who you are. This sheath of higher consciousness or spirituality is more challenging to explain because words can only point toward it. While this sheath can't be fully described, you can relate to it, because you've experienced it.

Nothing touches you as deeply or heals your anxiety more profoundly than this sheath. Experiences of deep connection, peace, and knowing, which this sheath accesses, let you know beyond any doubt that you're more than your body and your mind. Most everyone has had profound experiences of higher consciousness, whether or not they were recognized as such. Later in this chapter, we tell stories to help you remember times when you connected deeply to life so that you can reconnect to your tremendous depth and wholeness.

The Interrelationship of the Sheaths

In the same way that yeast is joined with flour to make bread, the five sheaths are inseparable. Since they're interconnected, the physical, energy, and mental sheaths reflect the condition of the others. Distress in one spreads through the others. That's why anxiety saturates body, energy, and mind. However, the higher forms of consciousness, the wisdom and bliss sheaths, don't suffer; rather, they infuse you with love and truth. Turn to them, become aware of them, and rely on them for your healing.

Suffering occurs in body, energy, and mind. And suffering opens you up to the realm of higher consciousness, because when you're on your knees and don't know what else to do, you turn to spiritual life. Exhausted by your everyday efforts to fix what seems to be broken, you seek comfort, understanding, and guidance just as you're doing in reading this book. You want relief from suffering, and are turning to the healing practices of yoga.

Mary's Healing

Mary had long suffered from a low level but ongoing state of anxiety. One spring her anxiety reached new heights and was unbearable at times. Although she didn't know when the symptoms would strike, she discovered that they amped way up when she wasn't busy. In her office, in between counseling sessions, her anxiety erupted. In her words, "It rose with a vengeance." During intense episodes, her body, mind, and energy were "consumed."

One day, during a state of high anxiety, she heard these words: *Get down on the floor!* She remembered having read some years earlier about a spiritual teacher who would lie on his back, with arms outstretched, and breathe through extreme anxiety. The man discovered that anxiety passed through him when he allowed it to do so rather than resist it. Although lying down on the floor seemed weird, Mary decided to give it a try. For the next few months, whenever she was anxious, she would lie down on the floor.

Here's what she discovered, in her words:

When I was on my back, not fighting the anxiety, I felt something. The anxiety was there, but I didn't feel lost in it. I focused on breathing in and out. With my attention on the breath, my mind quieted. I didn't react to the anxiety. It was as if some other energy arose to meet the anxiety. I call it presence. Whatever it was, it seemed stronger than anxiety. It was sweet and steady and alive. After some time, the anxiety subsided, and there I was, being held by this presence. I grew to love it. After some months, the acute anxiety left. My season of high anxiety passed, and so far, it hasn't come back. You know, I still lie on the floor, breathing in and out, and at times, I feel that same presence. Somehow, I feel connected. Lying on the floor, breathing in and out, is part of my spiritual practice.

Mary felt healed by the practice of lying on the floor, breathing, and surrendering—allowing her anxiety to be. She gave up attempts to control the anxiety or make it go away. Really, because she didn't know what else to do, she went to the floor. Looking back, she calls the practice "Breathe, allow, and simply be."

True Healing Involves All the Sheaths

True healing involves all the sheaths and can begin in any one of them. Understanding the powerful relationship of the bodies is important enough that we're giving another example. This time we look at how working with the energy body brought about healing. Because social phobia, or fear of public speaking, is the most widespread form of anxiety, we share Roberto's healing story.

Roberto's Healing

Roberto, a man in his mid fifties, was preparing to deliver a speech to a large audience. It was a great honor and he naturally wanted to do well, so he prepared and practiced. A week prior to giving his talk, he became highly anxious. He had anxiety medication and was willing to take it as needed, but wanted some other way to help himself on the day of the presentation. Here's his story:

> I'm a meditator, but meditating on breathing didn't calm me that week. I was too agitated. Then I remembered reading about meditating on the heart. The instruction was to breathe in and out of the heart. I tried, but that wasn't strong enough to slow my worrisome thoughts. In fact, breathing in and out of my heart actually hurt. I felt an ache there.
>
> I instinctively placed my hand over my heart to rub the ache. I was surprised at how soothing it was. I sat there, meditating, rubbing my heart with my hand. My heart felt warm beneath the touch of my hand. For the first time in days, my mind became quiet. I enjoyed the meditation and feeling the energy of my heart.
>
> Then it dawned on me, why not practice my presentation while touching my heart? So I did and I made some interesting discoveries: (1) When I felt my hand on my chest, I stayed in the present moment; I didn't race ahead of myself. (2) With my hand on my chest, breathing was

*comfortable, and my voice relaxed. (3) Aware of the warmth
of my heart, I felt supported. I knew my speech. I just had to
relax and stay in the present moment.*

By the way, Roberto didn't need medication to soothe his
anxiety on the day of his talk. Before leaving his hotel room to
present, he sat quietly with his hand over his heart, meditating. He
not only gave a great speech but also found a way to participate in
his own healing. When his body was soothed, his mind quieted.
When his breathing relaxed, so did his voice.

unity experiences

You may have had experiences when you felt utterly connected to
life. Perhaps it was when you held a sleeping baby and felt that
the two of you were inseparable, as if you were one being. Perhaps
it was when you walked in the wilderness and felt as if you were
part of it, or when you were walking in the early morning and the
silence you felt inside was inseparable from the profound silence of
the quiet neighborhood. If you've had these kinds of experiences,
you know that you felt deeply peaceful then.

Brad's Story

*Many years ago, while visiting Rocky Mountain National
Park, a small group of us went on an afternoon car ride. We
stopped at a turnout, and I felt compelled to walk away from
the group to stand alone, facing the immensity of the view. It
was cloudy, windy, and drizzling, and I was pelted with cold
raindrops. Suddenly, everything became quiet; there was only
vastness, timelessness, utter beauty, and indescribable peace.*

*My friends called me back to the car, and I reluctantly
turned toward them, feeling bereaved, as if I were leaving my*

beloved. I went, but silently. Something had been realized, although there were no words to articulate the experience. The inner silence was profound and compelling.

Since that time, silence has felt palpable. All I have to do is pause and listen, and I'm immersed in silence. Something changed in me that day. I don't feel alone; silence comforts me, reassures me that what I live and breathe in is alive and pervasive. That experience drew me into meditation and the spiritual life. My eyes stopped looking outside for sustenance; they began to turn inward, into the peace of the stillness within.

Brad's life slowly began to change. A workaholic for many years, he was the kind of guy you relied on to get the job done but not the one you turned to for laughter. After his experience in Colorado, he lost interest in working eighty hours a week and developed a love for hiking in the mountains. He began reading books on spirituality and went to yoga classes. The mystical experience on the mountaintop was a turning point in his life, bringing him in touch with higher consciousness.

It's not uncommon to be in the wilderness and experience this sense of unity and higher consciousness. Of course, mystical experiences can occur anytime, anywhere. Several years ago, while at a meditation retreat, a young college student had a powerful experience. During a walking meditation, he felt pulled to move away from the group and head toward the lake. At the end of the retreat, he shared with the group that he had experienced union with God while slowly strolling alone near the shore. He reported, "God is everywhere, omnipresent; I am not separate from God."

He had felt an indescribable joy, and added that the experience resolved his conflict about meditation. He had been attracted to meditation but concerned about stepping beyond the bounds of his conservative religious upbringing. In his words, "The peace that comes when my mind is quiet in meditation is the same as the peace I experienced walking near the shore."

Experiences of higher consciousness impact you. Sooner or later, they redirect your life. They turn your attention to the inner world of peace and contentment.

Children's Mystical Experiences

Mystical experiences occur for people of all ages. Children often have profound mystical experiences. Mary shares one of hers as a way of prompting your memory if you had a deeply spiritual experience as a child.

Mary's Story

When I was twelve, I visited a Catholic grotto with my mom and aunt on a cloudy, cold March day. I ducked into an enclosed area to be out of the wind, and was alone in a quiet room that represented the tomb of Christ. Standing beside the tomb was a statue of an angel with one arm outstretched in the direction of the tomb. I looked up at the statue and placed my hand in the concrete hand. I felt a surge of warmth, love, and understanding, as if I were not alone. Transfixed, I remained there, in deep communion. Then I heard footsteps and shyly retracted my hand before anybody saw. After that experience I loved being in the sanctuary during church services. I sat in a pew on the east side, next to a stained-glass window, where the sun's rays, streaming through the image of Christ, seemed to bathe me in compassion.

Like many other people, Mary had experienced trauma in her childhood and, previous to that experience, hadn't felt safe in her home. But after that visit to the grotto, she grew to love the solitude and peace in her bedroom. She felt comforted there, and somehow less alone.

PRACTICE: REMEMBERING UNITY EXPERIENCES

Do you recall any unity experiences? As you consider your experiences, recall possible moments when you were alone, listening to music, walking on the beach with a friend, or lying outside under the stars. Unity experiences can seem dramatic or ordinary, and can be fleeting or longer lasting. Write your story in a journal or tell it to someone you trust. Let yourself be touched by remembering, writing, and telling. Reclaim the truth that you belong, that you matter.

Profound Connection

Profound connection is a form of unity. You can feel this deep communion when rocking a sleeping child, stroking your beloved pet, tending to your garden, sitting with a dying loved one, watching the sun rise, and an infinite number of other ways. As this sense of connection arises, you recognize that words aren't needed, that you're contented with being quiet. You feel peaceful and utterly without anxiety.

Times of being "in the flow" are also experiences of unity. Whether you're jogging, dancing, drawing, or sculpting, there's a sense of timelessness and connectedness. You feel whole. Nothing is missing, and life feels okay as it is. Your thinking mind is totally immersed, with all its attention on the present-moment experience. It doesn't analyze, anticipate, or remember, so there's no anxiety.

PRACTICE: EXPLORE YOUR PROFOUND CONNECTION EXPERIENCES

Remember times of profound connection and experiences of being "in the flow." Tell your experiences to someone you trust or write about them in a journal. Let yourself be touched by remembering, writing, and telling. Rediscover that you're inexorably connected with life.

Near-Death Experiences

Other powerful events of higher consciousness, such as near-death experiences, can alter your sense of who you are and what matters to you. Near-death experiences, whether or not they're dramatic, remind you of your mortality. Following is a near-death experience that greatly impacted Rick. We're sharing it here to stir your memory.

Rick's Experience

Many years ago my girlfriend and I traveled in a third-world country, and I became extremely ill. I sought medical help, but the hospitals were dreadfully primitive. I had a cousin living in Istanbul, so I made my way there to seek medical care. By the time I got to Istanbul, my health was extremely precarious. Within minutes after arriving at my cousin's home, I collapsed on the floor in excruciating pain. I knew I was dying. As I slipped away from my body, I was no longer in pain. A profound peace came over me as I let go. Then I was up above my cousin, watching as he tried to bring me back to life. Outside of my body, looking down at my lifeless form, I felt alive, free of pain, incredibly still, and peaceful. I tried to comfort my loved ones as they cried in horror at my death, but they couldn't hear my words.

They made an urgent call and arranged for a doctor to make a house visit. While attempting to revive me, the physician did something that really provoked me. I felt angry and wanted to hit him. I was so determined that I focused all my energy to punch him in the nose. I raised my fist, and in what seemed like a few seconds later, I opened my eyes and looked around—but the doctor wasn't there; only my cousin and girlfriend were in the room. I felt no pain, sat up, and asked where the doctor was. After some time my cousin gained his composure and said, "The doctor left some twenty minutes ago. He had done all he could do and pronounced you dead."

That experience left a permanent impression on me. I knew that as a human being, I wasn't contained by my body. It changed my entire life. I gave up a profitable job, took up meditation, and got out of a love relationship that was comfortable but not right. That was some years ago. Still, today, I remember, and when I flounder, I schedule some time to go into nature. There, in the quiet, I remember the preciousness of life, that I am not my body. That remembering and clarity helps me to see through situations well enough to make important decisions.

Most everyone has had a brush with death. The deaths of beloved pets and intimate family members remind us that our bodies are temporary and that death is a fact of life. Close calls, nearly fatal accidents, and serious illness remind you that life is precious and that death can come at any time. Near-death experiences are wake-up calls. They remind you of what you already know, even if this knowing is deeply buried in unconsciousness.

What do you already know? Is it related to any of the following possible truths?

- I can't continue living this way; something doesn't feel real and true.

- I have to make significant changes for my health and happiness.

- There's more to life than how I've been living.

- I have to realign my life with what really matters to me.

- I need to listen to and follow my inner guidance.

PRACTICE: WAKE-UP CALLS

What wake-up calls have you had? How has death come close to you? How did the experiences realign your life with what's real and true? Did you act on the guidance you received? If not, can you now? Tell your experiences to someone you trust or write about them in a journal. Remember, your life is precious. How best might you honor and value this preciousness?

Spiritual Opening

A spiritual opening is an event, or series of events, that answers the question "who am I?" An experience of elevated consciousness, it shows you who you truly are. It shifts your perspective in such a way that you don't interpret life from the limited perspective of your conditioned identity. As a result, you experience all of life as sacred.

You still live in your body and have your mind with all its stories. An old story may tug at you, even toss you around a little, but then, miraculously, you see it, call it by its name, and smile at it. You realize that your old stories are the workings of a child's mind. Like a mother, you glance over to see what your child's mind is doing and then redirect your attention back to the present.

You turn to the blessed stillness for guidance instead of letting old stories make important decisions. You tap into the indwelling place of quiet and joy, not only because it feels wonderful but because you know it to be your true self and your true home.

Spiritual openings occur in little and big ways. There's one fundamental realization, whether it's a fleeting recognition or a lasting shift of consciousness. Any moment of recognition that you're awareness, consciousness, or spirit alters your sense of who you are. It's just that you may forget, but fortunately you can remember again.

Stephanie's Dream

God was in my head, showing me scenes from my childhood and talking to me, in my own voice. Many of the scenes were traumatic. Some of the scenes were of adults being kind to me. In every scene, God said, "I was there with you." The dream ended with God saying, again in my voice, "I am with you always; I will never forsake you."

Stephanie added that although she'd had the dream many years ago, it still powerfully impacted her. Then she said in a hushed voice, "There's no doubt that I'm a conscious being, that I'm loved, that I'm never alone.

PRACTICE: YOUR PRECIOUS SELF

What moments, dreams, and experiences left you with the awareness that you're a manifestation of consciousness or a child of God? How did they alter your sense of identity? Perhaps you heard a song or read a prayer and knew you were a sacred being, perhaps you felt a loving presence with you, or maybe you had a serious illness that left you with no doubt that you're more than your temporary body and mind. Tell your experiences to someone you trust or write about them. Let yourself remember again.

conclusion

The shift from anxiety to contentment occurs when compassion, insight, and deep connection permeate body, mind, and energy. True healing includes all five sheaths. Yoga practices are designed to make you conscious of not only your outer layer but also your innermost self. This chapter encouraged you to reconnect with your essence. As you continue your journey of healing, remember who you truly are. To deepen your insight into anxiety, we now move to an exploration of the underlying causes of anxiety.

chapter 4

a deeper look
at anxiety

When you enter into your suffering, a lot of the suffering is relieved.

—Father Basil Pennington

When you journey into the places of anxiety, you don't have to enter alone. You have breathing to steady you and witnessing to hold your hand. With these companions, you don't get lost. Supported, you can see, feel, and understand in ways that relieve your suffering. So that you can enter your places of anxiety, we look next at *kleshas*, which is Sanskrit for "afflictions." Considered to be the primary causes of human misery, there are five afflictions, all of which can lead to anxiety. As we discuss them, we invite you to inquire into possible ways they contribute to your anxiety.

ignorance (avidya)

Ignorance—simply "not knowing" (in Sanskrit, *avidya*)—is a foremost cause of misery. Everyone has experienced the painful consequences of making decisions based on missing or incomplete information. In the aftermath of such decisions, you shake your head and whisper, "I wish I had known." Decisions based on misunderstanding cause suffering. The greatest ignorance of all is mistaking the unreal for the real, that is, when you can't distinguish your self-limiting story from the deeper truth of who you are.

Human life is miraculous. You've undoubtedly been awed by the innocent beauty of infants, sensing that they're a cherished gift of life. Amazingly, you may overlook that your life is just as miraculous. Nearly all of us fall under the spell of spiritual ignorance and forget who we are. When the knowledge that you are sacred slips into unconsciousness, all that's left is the mundane. Your sense of who you are is reduced to thoughts, ideas, body parts, and things, which are ever changing and transitory, and you inevitably feel somehow incomplete and discontented. You have to search for happiness, because you don't experience it in yourself.

Not sensing your spiritual essence, you have no safe haven, no inner place of comfort. When you don't know that you *are* spirit or consciousness, deep within, you feel an existential aloneness that causes tremendous anxiety. And when you do sense your essence, you feel contented and happy for no reason.

Not knowing who you are causes you to experience yourself as bereft of the spiritual, as it did Ben.

Ben's Story

Several months after Ben, aged fifty, left his partner of fifteen years, he knew he had to make some changes. During the last decade of his relationship, he had drunk more and more wine to cope with a relationship that was dreadfully undernourishing and draining. Wine had numbed him to his own emotional needs, dulling his worries and anxiety. Ben had hoped he could stop drinking after exiting the relationship, but nearly a year later, most evenings he was still drinking. Determined to be happier, he began attending Alcoholics Anonymous (AA) and gradually reduced his drinking. Although he felt better physically and could think more clearly, his anxiety mounted.

He stopped attending AA, because participating brought up his struggles with spirituality. He didn't know what kind of god to believe in and felt spiritually malnourished. Half panicky, half determined, he started taking a couple of yoga classes weekly at his church. He loved the sense of connection and peace he felt at the end of class, when everyone sat in quiet meditation. He eventually stopped drinking, but as time went on, it became apparent to him that his recovery had to include a sense of belonging with others and with life. He relied more and more on meditative yoga and fishing at the river.

Today Ben feels better yet still struggles with accepting his own inner preciousness. He knows beyond doubt that his daughter is a divine child of the universe, that his pet dog is "God incarnate," and that the troubled teenagers he works with are precious. At least now, he realizes the discrepancy between how he experiences others and how he experiences himself. Slowly, gradually, he's finding his way into his own sacred goodness. He also finds solace sitting on the bank of the river, where he feels connected to what he calls "the great life force."

PRACTICE: EXPLORING IGNORANCE

Here are questions to guide you in exploring ignorance. Give yourself plenty of time to answer so you'll be carried beyond superficial answers into a more revealing exploration.

- How does my physical body determine my sense of self-worth?

- How does my appearance affect my anxiety?

- How does my status in outer life determine my sense of self?

- How does my status affect my anxiety?

- How is my sense of self impacted when I "fail" or "succeed"?

- When do I most experience the sacred?

- When can I give myself quiet time to rejuvenate and reflect?

- Write about an experience that was spiritually nourishing.

limited self-concept (asmita)

Limited self-concept (or in Sanskit, *asmita*) is when we mistakenly believe the self-limiting stories we tell ourselves: "I'm an anxious person," "I'm an angry person, "I'm a sad person," and so on. This form of suffering is caused by not challenging the old ideas and stories you tell yourself.

You know that you're in the grips of limited self-concept when you hear yourself say, "I've always been like this; I can't change. This is just the way I am." Asmita is the seal of "innocent misunderstanding," believing the old story of identity.

PRACTICE: EXPLORING LIMITED SELF-CONCEPT

Inquire into your limited self-concept. Complete each sentence seven times. Then identify which beliefs are most central to how you experience yourself. Write your answers in a journal or discuss them with someone you trust.

- I limit myself by believing that I _____.

- I don't believe that I can _____.

- It doesnt seem possible that I could actually _____.

Now go back over your answers and circle the limiting beliefs that you sense hold you back the most.

Limited self-concept can be disputed. You can put all your fixed ideas about who you are and what you can and can't do to the test. It's a simple test that consists of this question: Is this belief really true?

PRACTICE: BREAKING FREE

To break free from your historical sense of self, lovingly confront your limiting beliefs. Go back to the limiting beliefs you circled in the previous practice. With the kindness of a loving grandmother, ask yourself the following questions:

- "How many years have I been saying this?"

- "Is this belief really true?"

- "Do I know for sure that this is true?"

- "What does the data say?"

Simply asking the questions brings awareness. You don't have to reframe the story, make up a better story, or fix it in any way. By simply becoming aware of the story, you let go of its unconscious influence over you.

Here's an example of how one woman in her mid thirties challenged a story she had carried over from childhood into adulthood.

Bettianne's Story

Bettianne often said, "I'm just a poor girl from Chicago." It's true that Bettianne was raised in poverty. However, she carried that story of limited self-concept around many years after she left her home state and was working as a professional in another city. Because Bettianne believed that she was *just* (implying merely or only), she suffered from chronic anxiety. She didn't feel equal to her professional colleagues. Insecure and shy, she felt like an imposter. She worried that her superiors would appraise her the same way she assessed herself, as not measuring up with others. Bettianne received top ratings on her annual evaluations and was well respected by her work associates. Although who she was in essence was worth far more than her successes, even her current status suggested that she was "good enough" by societal standards. Yet her unexamined belief asserted that she was not.

Here's how she confronted her belief. She would say, "I'm just a poor girl from Chicago," and then refute it with the actual data: "I live in a city, I earn a professional salary, my home is in a middle-class neighborhood, I got a promotion, and my colleagues ask for and respect my opinion. I'm not a girl; I'm in my thirties." She concluded each encounter with these contradictions between her old self-concepts and the present facts of her life by laughing, breathing a sigh of relief, and emphatically saying, "Yes!"

Bettianne asked the question, "Is this self-concept really true?" hundreds of times. The question became part of her therapeutic practice, especially after she began reaping its benefits. She loved "busting" her belief of inferiority that had once seemed so solidly cemented in her psyche. Doing so had the effect of opening her up to a deeper sense of being, because she realized she was just as precious when she was poor as she was now, that her essential goodness was and had always been unrelated to her social status.

Living in Chicago poverty was part of her conditioning, not who she actually was. You, like her, aren't your conditioning. Yes, your past affected you, but you can't be reduced to the effects of your conditioning. On the other hand, until you become conscious of your self-concepts and their relationship to the past, you're greatly impacted by the environmental and formative effects of your early life.

attachment (raga)

Another klesha is attachment, or *raga*, which is the fearful holding on to something pleasurable or desired. The energy of attachment is like a hand that clings and grasps into a tight fist. Attachment isn't about "who" you think you are; rather, it's about what you think you need in order to be okay. It's the sense that you have to have a certain something to make your life okay. When you hear yourself say, "I have to have," "I'd die without," or "It has to be," you're in the grips of attachment.

Attachment has a definite sticky emotional quality of urgency. The emotional charge is strong. Attachment is not just believing something; it's clinging desperately to something. Attachments are well defined, specific: "I need this relationship," "I need this kind of job," "I need to know."

PRACTICE: KNOW YOUR ATTACHMENTS

To discover what you're attached to, do an inquiry. Complete each sentence seven times. You may find that you move past more superficial attachments into deeper, less conscious ones. You may uncover a core story about yourself or a powerful belief that you weren't aware of that contributes to anxiety.

- I have to have _____.

- I feel as if I would die without _____.

- It has to be that _____.

The Brain and Attachment

In his book *Light on The Yoga Sūtras of Patañjali*, B. K. S. Iyengar (1993) wrote that attachment is associated with the hypothalamus in the brain. This almond-shaped gland, located deep within the brain, controls many bodily functions, including blood pressure, heart rate, and body temperature, and is a coordinator of the autonomic nervous system. Highly sensitive to emotional stress, the hypothalamus responds to threats, real or imagined, by sending out hormonal messages. This process, which triggers the fight-or-flight response, bypasses the logical, thinking part of the brain.

Attachment, being associated with the hypothalamus, bypasses reason. Now you can appreciate the strong emotional charge attachment has. Attachment is so powerful that in the book *Yoga and Psychotherapy* (Swami Rama, Ballentine, and Ajaya 1976), Swami Rama refers to it as the primary cause of anxiety.

Attachment to Certainty and Control

When you worry about and are preoccupied with the future, you want certainty, because you're trying to figure out what's going to happen in the future so that you can be prepared for it and thus be in control. Additionally, when you clamp down on your emotions, you exert great effort to be in control of yourself. You don't want to appear weak, feel vulnerable, or experience unpleasant emotions, so you endeavor to keep yourself in your safety zone. Keeping safe and secure is a survival response, but feeling that you *need* to always appear strong and invulnerable is another thing.

Let's look at phobias and how they pertain to attachment to certainty. A *phobia* is an irrational, excessive, and persistent fear of some particular thing or situation. An irrational fear of elevators, flying in airplanes, public speaking, driving alone when road conditions are safe, and so on greatly limits you when you allow it to be a primary driving force in your decision making. It's one thing to have such a fear and another to let it control your lifestyle, which it does when your need to be in control of your emotions causes you to steer clear of doing activities you might otherwise enjoy and find beneficial.

Nearly everyone is attached to control and certainty at some level. True healing from anxiety involves seeing and acknowledging our underlying attachment to control and certainty. Let's apply this to recovery from trauma, since trauma is not only a frequent cause of anxiety but also is experienced by most people at some time in their lives.

The aftermath of trauma inevitably includes a movement toward control and certainty. How could it not? If we've slipped on the stairs and hurt ourselves, we negotiate those stairs more carefully in the future. If we've been badly injured in a car accident, we may be more careful in the future when we drive. If someone in our lives has betrayed us, we may avoid having anything to do with that person in the future. Trauma, by its nature, shatters our sense of safety. In the same way that an animal goes to its den to recover, you retreat to whatever places inside yourself, as well as in the outer world, feel the most secure to you.

Accordingly, after physical injury, it's therapeutic to strengthen your physical body through rest, good nutrition, and exercise. In the aftermath of emotional injuries, it's healing to develop boundaries with people, ideas, and situations that are harmful to you. Both strategies are necessary for your recovery and help you rebuild your sense of safety. But healing doesn't end there; it also includes learning to tolerate uncertainty, because as we all know, life offers no guarantees of constant safety and security. Healing involves becoming able to deal with the inevitable anxiety that accompanies moving on and keeping our hearts open. As you read on, you'll find many specific ways to help you deal with intense fear and anxiety, such as the comfort pose to reduce emotional upset described in chapter 6.

Absence of Attachment

To understand this more thoroughly, let's look at the absence of attachment, or nonattachment, which entails living contentedly with uncertainty. As you know, life's not static; it changes and moves. The absence of attachment is accepting life as it is.

It's not so easy to do! Our minds recoil from letting go and letting life be as it is. We don't want to acknowledge that our ideas about how we think life should be contribute to our stress. (By the way, you're not "wrong" in seeking control; this reflex is an extension of the survival instinct of protection. Some would say it's simply your ego doing its job, attempting to protect you.) Yet it's healing to acknowledge that you inevitably think and feel that life should be other than it is. Simply admitting your desire for control releases its grip on you and helps you deal with life, especially with things you wish weren't happening.

Accepting "what is" is the heart of nonattachment, and includes recognizing what's happening inside of you as well as what's happening in the outer world. Accepting "what is" includes all your thoughts and emotional reactions to events that occur around you. Acceptance doesn't necessarily mean approving of or liking; it implies recognizing what's actually occurring and finding a way to live more comfortably with life as it is. Nor does it mean passive noninvolvement. In fact, you make empowered choices when you're aware of what's occurring. For example, acknowledging that you're thinking, *I don't like what's happening; I'm scared*, and then taking a deep breath or two so you don't get lost in your emotions, helps you assess whether or not there's anything you can do about the situation.

Denying "what is" is the opposite of nonattachment. Denial is the most powerful psychological defense mechanism, so let's give it our due respect. Accepting things that happen, how you feel, and what you think are no small tasks. And yet, true healing asks you to, and you can, with the help of your companions, breathing and witnessing, and many other yoga practices.

Engaging in meditation, inquiry, devotional prayer, and mantra (reciting a wise or sacred word or phrase), as well as reading your favorite sacred scriptures, helps you to accept life as it is. These practices connect you with higher consciousness so you can say, "Let go and let God," or some other phrase that appeals to you, and ride the wave of your anxious feelings. Breathing and witnessing, you can let such feelings move through you without them retraumatizing you.

Janette's healing story shows the power of nonattachment in recovering from emotional and physical trauma.

Janette's Story

Janette is a beautiful and good-natured woman. She was physically abused as a child and witnessed her father physically abuse her mother. Over the years it seemed as if her mother's life force withered, and she died of cancer in her early forties. Devastated by her mother's death, Janette turned to food to cope. She hit bottom at age thirty-six and began attending Overeaters Anonymous. Her food binges subsided, but she began experiencing panic attacks and anxiety. In addition to her 12-step program, she started counseling, took yoga classes, and attended meditation retreats.

Now, eight years later, she credits Overeaters Anonymous, yoga, and meditation for her recovery. She says:

> When I'm anxious, I say to myself, "Breathe and let it be." I
> go to yoga class faithfully and am learning to relax my body, I
> practice witnessing my fearful thoughts, and I get on my knees
> daily to pray not only for the strength to accept life as it is but
> also for the ability to enjoy life as it is.

As Janette discovered when she went into recovery, all the emotions she had anesthetized with food were still there. She thought she couldn't deal with her grief from her mother's death or the underlying trauma and anxiety about the physical abuse she had witnessed and experienced as a child. But with the support of yoga, meditation, and prayer, she found that she could feel her emotions without getting lost in them. She said:

> I felt like I was blind before recovery. Now I can see. Yes, I
> still tremble at times, but I don't feel lost in darkness. I can
> see my scared thoughts and feel the old anxiety. I can keep my

eyes open. Well, at least when I realize that I've shut my eyes, I can breathe, open them, and take a look. And, I'm having a lot more fun with life these days.

PRACTICE: EXPLORING ATTACHMENT TO CERTAINTY AND CONTROL

Look into your attachments by completing each sentence seven times. You may find that you move past more superficial attachments into deeper, less conscious ones. Write your answers in a journal or talk with a trusted person.

- How do I attempt to keep myself safe?

- What do I try to control?

- What do I like to be certain of?

- How do I use food, shopping, information, sex, drugs and alcohol, exercise, excessive work, and personal relationships for security or safety?

Since attachment is considered a primary cause of anxiety, we'll cover it in more depth by exploring the attachment to perfection.

Attachment to Being Perfect

Perfectionism is a force that stomps on compassion and squelches happiness. A relentless pressure, perfectionistic thinking doesn't have a clue about your inherent value, so it gives you strict guidelines about how to make yourself into a *good-enough* somebody. No wonder it's closely linked to anxiety. If you suffer from wanting to be perfect, you have recurring thoughts about following rules; meeting high expectations; and reinforcing rigid, moralistic standards. With perfectionism as a driving force in your life, you may believe that you can earn and reinforce your self-worth by following

87

strict guidelines and achieving very specific results. As you read on, consider whether you have tendencies toward perfectionism. You may have a few of the traits or suffer from more pervasive perfectionism. Either way, it may contribute to your anxiety.

In *Too Perfect* Allan E. Mallinger and Jeannette DeWyze (1992) explain that perfectionists need to feel in control at all times to feel safe. They fear coloring outside the lines and work hard to comply with self-imposed standards, often ones they don't fully understand. Through vigilance and great effort, perfectionists attempt to get it right. Can you sense the tension this creates? This tension, which is shared by so many of us, can be paralyzing, making us afraid to attempt anything that we or others might judge.

Perfectionism and Addiction

If you suffer from perfectionism, you may be addicted to work, having a perfect body, or being a perfect person. These addictions reveal the inner pressure to "get it right." The workaholic focuses on work productivity or excellence. The perfect-body addict seeks a set body weight and clothing size. And the perfect-person addict imposes rigid moral and social codes. Meeting the standards takes precedence over everything else, including enjoying life and relationships with others. The urgent pressure to be perfect and the resulting isolation can cause high and chronic anxiety—and cause you to be less and less aware of your sacred essence.

Perfectionism and Criticism

If you're perfectionistic, you're probably both highly sensitive to criticism and critical of others. In fact, the hallmark of perfectionism is being critical. Criticizing yourself feels familiar, even helpful, as a motivator to do better. Hearing criticism from others, though, can tap into your underlying belief that you're flawed. Criticism feels shaming and paralyzing, which stops you in your tracks and prevents you from trying new things, doing anything creative, or taking interpersonal risks.

Some perfectionists are passive and do everything they can to be invisible, to avoid being seen or having attention drawn to them. Others, because of their impeccable appearance and performance, may look good to others. Although perfectionism is painful and causes high anxiety, other people may not see the perfectionist's suffering. On the outside, it may look as though you're highly motivated and in charge.

Shelly's Story

Shelly, a beautiful woman in her late thirties, came to Mary's office for counseling for help with chronic anxiety a few years after her husband had died. Underneath Shelly's slender, fit, and carefully dressed body, her posture seemed rigid and her face was tense. Nervous and shy, she focused on her work and adhered to a rigorous exercise schedule and strict dietary protocol. Shelly had dated since her husband's death, but the relationships hadn't lasted. Friendships and love relationships were not nurturing for Shelly, so she turned away from them.

Shelly's mother had died when she was an infant, and her father had traveled extensively for business. When he was gone, she stayed with various aunts and uncles. She adapted to living in numerous homes by becoming the perfect child—compliant, pleasing, and undemanding—as her need for nurturance gave way to her need for stability and security. Bright and dutiful, she had found self-worth through academic excellence, and then inevitably carried that pattern into adulthood. She equated high achievement with being good enough, which set her up for perfectionism. By the time she was an adult, her self-talk was highly critical, and she postponed going to graduate school for fear of failing. When friends and lovers were critical of her, she thought it was somehow her fault. She worked harder to do better.

Over time Shelly began to understand that she believed the story, "Nobody's there for me." She was anxious because she didn't know that, as a human being, she was already precious. Her gravitation toward perfection was an attempt to create a sense of self in being a good-enough person. Prone to headaches and a nervous stomach, she looked good on the outside but felt anxious on the inside. Shelly stayed busy; tried hard to be pretty, although she felt unattractive; and kept her emotions under cover. Her pain was invisible and she suffered in silence.

Shelly's healing was gradual, but there was a pivotal moment. One day she cried out in pain, "I'm so lonely. Isn't there something I can do to help myself?" Miserable, she covered her face with her hands and wept. Mary encouraged Shelly to place her hand over her heart and to breathe compassion into her pain. While Shelly gently patted her heart, Mary instructed her to whisper, "I am here for me." They sat for some time while Shelly patted her heart and recited her loving self-talk as a mantra.

Shelly agreed to touch her heart and whisper, "I am here for me," nightly, before going to sleep. She was faithful to her practice, and within weeks her anguish began to subside. Over the next couple of years, she deepened her friendships with others, exercised less compulsively, adopted a more casual appearance, and dared to go to graduate school, where she met a man who was genuinely interested in her. In a recent conversation with Mary, Shelly said, "I still do my self-loving practice. I'm much kinder to myself in general, and although I feel anxious at times, I feel okay being me."

aversion (dvesa)

Aversion (in Sanskrit, *dvesa*) is the flip side of attachment. For every attachment, there's an aversion; for everything you cling to, there's something from which you recoil. Aversion is the impulse to avoid or move away from something, whether it's a person, activity, object, or idea. You're in the grips of aversion when you say, "I can't bear this," "I couldn't possibly deal with it," "I can't stand such and such," or "I have a sick feeling at the sight or thought of this." Associated with the hypothalamus in the same way that attachment is, aversion is a powerful energy that triggers a feeling of endangerment or intense insecurity when you're not actually faced with an imminent threat to your safety. Of course, you naturally move away from something that's really potentially harmful, such as driving the wrong way on a one-way road during rush-hour traffic, beginning the instant you see oncoming traffic until you get yourself and your vehicle off the road or safely turned around.

Like attachment, aversion is a reinforcing set of reactions between thinking and the body's stress response. As such, it can become a vicious cycle. The hypothalamus triggers the body's fight-or-flight response based on the mind's saying, *I can't bear.* The mind then judges the physical discomfort as intolerable, which in turn escalates the stress response.

Feel it yourself, if you like. Just for a moment, imagine that something's happening that you're averse to, such as giving a public presentation or being told your zipper's down. If the thought of these things happening triggers even a mild aversion, notice how your body revs up just a little. Your heart beats a little harder and you may squirm.

This is just an exercise. What you dread isn't actually happening, though you are imagining it in your mind. Yet even thinking about it or recalling unpleasant images causes the stress response. This uncomfortable exercise shows how aversion is created. Aversion is something that you think you can't bear or that you know could threaten your well-being if it actually happened.

One of the more anxiety-producing aversions is the thought of living on after someone dear to you dies. Most people recoil from this notion. It seems unbearable. Even considering the possibility causes agony, triggering an aversion to discussing it, seeing a film about it, reading about it, or even going to a friend's funeral.

Susan's Story

Susan sought counseling five months after her husband of thirty-five years committed suicide. She loved her husband and was devastated by his death. Many times she told Mary, "I cannot bear this; I feel dead inside. I want to be with him." The prospect of waking up yet another morning to find that he wasn't beside her was terrifying.

The counseling office became a safe place for her to grieve and to face the unbearable. For months she came to her weekly session and wept. At some point during each session, she moaned, "I can't do this; I can't live without him." Gently, Mary responded with, "Susan, I don't know how you're doing it, but you are bearing what you think you can't. Another week has gone by and here you are." Achingly, still in the early stages of overwhelming grief, she was facing what she thought she could not, the prospect of life without her husband. She was experiencing the inescapable aversion that's an aspect of bereavement.

No one wants to face traumatic death, yet many people outlive someone they love dearly. You know from your own experience that when life presents great challenge, you can only meet it moment by moment. Any movement away from the present moment can be excruciating. And while thoughts that this is more than you can bear are inevitable, seeing the thoughts for what they are helps you to breathe through the overwhelming anxiety that accompanies them. *I cannot bear* is a thought about what's too much for you in the next second and in the next day. You, like Susan, can only face whatever happens in your life as it occurs, moment by moment by moment.

Grief does not inhibit new life. As anyone who has been bereaved knows, initially grief is intense and all consuming. During the early stage of grief, new life doesn't come. But as time goes on, it's not just grief that interferes with reengaging with life but aversion—to letting go of the life that seemed so dear, to feeling vulnerable, to allowing grief to be felt, to risking again, and to moving on.

Susan's life moved on. In her final session she said, "You know, Mary, early on, when you said, 'You're bearing what you think you cannot bear,' I winced and even thought you were insensitive. Yet, the words were the truth. They reverberated in my mind and kept me going."

Underlying aversion is a lack of faith in your capacity to meet life circumstances as they change and move. Yet many of you have faced what you thought you couldn't face and lived through what you thought you couldn't. You face things and go on, because you have to, just as Susan did.

PRACTICE: EXPLORING AVERSIONS

Inquire into your aversions by completing each of the following sentences seven times. Give yourself some time to respond. Write whatever answers come up to let yourself move past superficial into deeper, less conscious aversions. Be gentle, because you may uncover a powerful belief that contributes to anxiety.

- I can't stand _____.

- I couldn't bear the thought of _____.

- I can't deal with _____.

fear of death (abhinivesha)

The fifth cause of misery, fear of death (or *abhinivesha*), is another expression of clinging to what is. You've probably attempted to revitalize something lifeless—such as an old friendship or the love you once had for a certain activity, lifestyle, or job—when you knew it was time to let go. If you've ever found yourself in that situation, you know how anxiety producing it can be. An obvious example of this is holding on to youth. Clinging to a youthful appearance causes anxiety, because it represents a denial of the seasons of human life. It's a misunderstanding of the way human life is.

The fear of death is associated with the amygdala, the part of the brain whose job is to ensure survival of the organism, the part that registers threat and takes action to defend and preserve life. Even though your body instinctually wants to live, it is finite. The human body, like all life forms that are born, dies. Everything associated with human life, our experiences and our relationships, is transitory. They live and then they die.

Fear of Loving

Fear of death is often transformed into a fear of loving. Psychologically, the fear of loving again after someone close to you has died is an aversion. You may think you can't bear to let go and love again knowing that you'll risk losing someone again and grieving all over again.

It's our human nature to love. Love is universal and knows no bounds; it's only the human mind that creates limitations around love. To think that we can love only one person, pet, object, lifestyle, or phase of life is a misunderstanding of the way life is. We don't know how long we'll live, or how long those we love will be with us or love us in return. In fact, realizing that we are all only on earth for a while helps us to treasure our loved ones and keep from taking them for granted. Most of us fall short of loving others or ourselves so openly, so the real healing move is to compassionately embrace it all, even our holding back from love.

Losses such as death, divorce, disability, and disaster aren't easy to deal with, nor is letting go of youth and material success in a culture that reveres both. Loss hurts. It takes time to heal and accept your suffering. Deep grief is a powerful energy that initially feels relentless and then later comes in waves. Metaphorically, and sometimes literally, it can drop you to your knees.

To say that you'll never love again due to the pain of grief is unfortunate because of the self-limitations it sets in motion. If you've lost a pet, you know this intimately. The grief that accompanies the death of a beloved animal can be intense. The only way through the grief is to let yourself feel it, knowing that grief is an aspect of love. Through its expression, your heart remains open, enabling you to bond with another animal. In a similar manner, people move in and out of your life. Saying, "I don't know if I can love again," during the early phases of grief gives you time to mourn. But, in the long haul, saying, "I'll never love again because endings hurt too much," cuts you off from life and your loving nature.

PRACTICE: EXPLORING THE FEAR OF DEATH

Inquire into your fear of death by completing the following sentences. Do an investigation. Be curious. Complete each sentence seven times so that you can go beyond the most obvious or superficial fears. Writing what you hear without editing may help you uncover deeper beliefs that cause anxiety.

Explore what you're holding onto that's fleeting, dying, or dead:

- I can't let go of _____.

- I have a hard time accepting that _____.

- I can't imagine going on living if _____.

- I'm hanging onto _____.

Marsha's Story

Marsha came to Mary's office for counseling after her only son, a teenager, died from a drug overdose. Her grief was intense and so was her fear. Some days she was so paralyzed with anxiety that she couldn't imagine ever facing the world again. However, she did. After a few months she returned to her job on a part-time basis, and after the initial adjustment she found the distraction of work relieving. Gradually she resumed full-time responsibility.

Ten months after her son died, she had an opportunity to move to Southern California to advance her career. The new job sounded interesting to her and included a significant salary increase. She was terrified to leave her friends yet felt that the move was the right step. She had been advised to avoid making significant changes during the first year of bereavement, and cautious by nature, she didn't want to make a big mistake. Then one day, she knew she would go and told Mary, "I wasn't ready for my son's death, but it happened anyway. I don't know if I'm ready to move on, but life doesn't wait until we're ready."

Mary saw Marsha seven months later, when she made a return trip to the area. Reporting that the move still felt right, Marsha said, "At times the grief still seems overwhelming, but I get up and go about my day. At least I'm less anxious. I'm grateful for the intellectual challenge of my work, and I enjoy my colleagues." She concluded the visit by commenting, "You know, I don't talk about it anymore, but part of me wonders why I'm still here. However, like it or not, life goes on, and I'm learning to accept that." She paused, and then added, "And I never thought I would say this again, but I do have moments of happiness."

Marsha's story is gripping. It seems painfully intimate, too close for comfort. You know this could easily happen to you. In fact, you probably know someone who has had a similar experience, or perhaps something equally compelling has happened to you. We share Marsha's story to give you a companion on the journey so that you can turn your face into the wind and meet life as it is.

Marsha developed a sacred practice to support her, and you can too.

Here's what Marsha did. She made her bedroom her sanctuary, complete with sacred objects: soft pillows, her son's shoes, and a rosary. For several months she retreated to her safe haven after work. Living with friends for the first eight months, she came out of her room when dinner was ready and then walked the dog before retreating back into her room. She ate her "love" food every day: one chocolate chip cookie baked by her best friend. She read a daily devotional reading and wrote in her journal every night.

Fear of Abandonment

As an aspect of the fear of death, we want to address a less obvious but very powerful fear. The fear of abandonment is a psychological fear that seems linked to physical survival. You hear this fear in phrases such as "I feel that I would die if he left me," "I can't make it on my own," "I need her," and "I can't be alone."

Underlying this fear is the belief that you're only okay, or safe, when you hold onto what you presently have. While it's easy to understand the instinctual need for physical safety, here we're talking about psychological safety. This painful fear confuses emotional support from a specific person with physical survival itself.

Let's add a little perspective. It's normal to have dependency needs, healthy to rely on loved ones for emotional support, and natural to form close bonds with others. It's not unusual to have some fear of being left behind. Fear of abandonment goes beyond normal adult human interdependency. At its roots, this is a deep belief that you can't survive on your own, without the support of this other person. As a result, you may fear desertion or betrayal and perhaps even see signs of rejection where there are none. This can also show up as fear of intimacy, stemming from the belief that the best way to prevent your experience of abandonment is to avoid getting too close in the first place.

Let's be compassionate as we look into this fear. Countless people suffer from fear of abandonment in varying degrees. This fear often stems from memories of childhood experiences of being abandoned or neglected, physically or emotionally. Abandonment in childhood can have long-lasting effects, because children need a caretaker's protection, love, and reassurance. Without physical shelter, children become weak; without emotional support, children's emotional development withers; and without touch, tiny infants usually pass away.

If your anxiety takes the form of the fear of abandonment, your hope for recovery rests in recognizing what's going on. If you have this fear, you may recognize some of the following: anxiety even at the thought of being alone, becoming anxious unless you receive constant reassurance, reaching out for intimacy inappropriately, suspecting betrayal without evidence that it's occurring, panicking over small indiscretions, indulging in emotional blackmail that can be expressed as "I'll hurt myself if you leave," or some combination of these. If you become aware of the form your anxiety is taking, you'll no longer unconsciously be held captive by the spell of this painful fear. If your anxiety takes any of these forms, know that you're not alone. If fear of abandonment is great, you may benefit from professional counseling. Additionally, you can help yourself with yoga practices.

Recognizing Fear of Abandonment

Be very gentle in acknowledging this fear. See it, face it, and look at it. Remember, becoming conscious of it is the first step toward freedom from anxiety. Give yourself some credit. While the support of others is necessary, they're not always available to you. However, you're always available to you, and you can learn to be supportive of yourself. You don't have to abandon yourself. As a starter, breathe deeply and whisper, "I am here, for myself; I am here."

As you go through this book, try the practices on and sense which ones work for you. Explore how you could personalize them to make them feel just right for you. Then claim your individualized yoga practice as your own, knowing that you can adjust it when you want to. Turn to your practices and rely on them, and they'll not only become as dear as a trusted friend but will also provide skills that see you through your storms.

conclusion

There are five causes of suffering:

- Ignorance of truth

- Limited self-concept

- Attachment

- Aversion

- Fear of death

It's helpful to look at them separately so that you can see how the root causes of anxiety live in you. However, they're all interrelated and mutually influence one another. Attachment, a powerful cause of anxiety, results from our efforts to hold onto what we think we need in order to feel okay. It's related to ignorance, because when we don't know who we are, we have to have something to cling to in order to feel empowered.

Now that you have some sense about the underlying causes of anxiety and how it lives in you, it's time to delve more deeply into the yoga practices that calm your anxious mind.

chapter 5

practices for calming your mind

Human beings, when not stressed, are utterly beautiful. It's only when we are confused that our hearts shrivel and our minds figure crafty ways out of situations…. When we relate to life from our minds, we take our feet off the ground. It's like not wanting to touch the floor, fearing that we will be burned.

—Stephen Levine

Our minds do the best they can as they try to protect us and help us navigate through our days. The mind doesn't have a clue that it keeps us fearful and unhappy, yet it does. In this chapter we take you step by step through practices that empower you to put your anxious thoughts to rest and awaken your capacity to fulfill your truest desires. You don't have to remain an innocent victim of anxiety-producing thoughts. You can shape your life by using your inner guidance and your loving heart as you learn to tap into them and follow them where they take you.

Since fear-producing thoughts often fly beneath the radar screen of our awareness, we don't even know they're influencing us. Well, they are, and here's an amazing promise. Not only can you become aware of your thoughts, but you can also literally fill your mind with thoughts that will help you actualize your human potential. In fact, the promise of this chapter is not just relief from anxiety but also the comfort and joy that come from being fully alive while keeping your feet on the ground.

becoming conscious in the present moment

Let's start with the obvious that isn't so obvious. All of life, including the experiences of anxiety and joy, takes place in the present moment. You anticipate the future in the present moment, which is what you're doing when you stew about something that hasn't yet happened. In the present moment you wring your hands over what might happen. Generally, all of your experience feels real, even if it's totally unrelated to what's actually happening in the physical reality outside of you.

Let's say you're nestled in your bed and dozing off to sleep at 10:30 p.m., when the phone rings. You wonder if something's wrong, and your heart skips a beat as you reach toward the nightstand to answer the phone. Nervous, you answer, and it's a wrong number. Relieved that it's not bad news, you hang up and curl back up in your bed. Your fear wasn't caused by the phone's ringing; it was caused by your internal response to it.

If you're like most people, it may seem as if you have no control over such fears, that they just wash over you. You can learn to be increasingly aware of your fearful and worrisome thoughts from moment to moment, and learn to relate to your anxiety, and even lessen it, so you can deal with things that actually happen. When you worry, you're lost in thought and robbed of the possibility of focusing on what you really want or on constructive problem solving.

imprints on the mind (samskaras)

Recurring thoughts, ideas, and behaviors carve deeply ingrained ruts or grooves into our minds. Called *samskaras* in the Yoga tradition, these imprints have a strong gravitational pull that can be difficult to resist over time. Samskaras can have a positive influence on your life, such as when you have healthy habits, or they can be damaging, such as when you repeat self-destructive behaviors that keep you trapped in a painful rut.

Samskaras are formed through repetition. Every time you repeat a thought or duplicate a behavior, you cut more deeply into its groove in your mind, reinforcing it as a habit (Forbes 2004, 2008). Each worrisome thought about whether or not someone likes you scratches into the apprehension indentation *What if people don't like me?* As the groove gets deeper, it becomes a more powerful force that leads to future actions or, in this case, more worries. In other words, your thoughts and behaviors not only mark your mind but also coalesce as impressions that lead to future actions.

As Georg Feuerstein states in *The Yoga Tradition* (1998, 320), samskaras live in your subconscious as "subliminal activators" that shape your thoughts, feelings, and actions in the world. As you can sense, they have tremendous power over you; they even determine the circumstances of your future life, if you let them continue to work on you subconsciously. Your old core stories are firmly entrenched samskaras; so are old trauma memories and persistent worrisome thoughts. Fortunately, the effect of becoming aware of them, when they arise, is equally powerful. Identify and witness your old stories, and over time, your grooves smooth out, which frees you from repeating self-destructive habits.

Neuroscience is verifying the yogic view of the mind's samskaras. In *The Mind and the Brain* (2002), Jeffrey Schwartz and Sharon Begley reported that scientists have found that the action of repeated firings of neurons changes the wiring of the brain. This means that you can change your mental wiring by what you think and how often you think it. Repeated anxious thoughts dig deep grooves. Let them run away with you, and they create ruts that are hard to get out of. Fortunately, calming and encouraging thoughts also carve tracks into your brain, developing your capacity to be calmer, even when you encounter life's rough spots.

Before proceeding, we want to point out that we've simplified the process of how patterns are formed in the brain so that you can work with your own "pattern making." In case what we're saying sounds mechanistic, we want to add that the process involves a miraculous synergy of literally billions of brain cells firing and forming associations with one another. Science can't fully explain what happens, because while your brain's electrical activity can be measured, the specific activity can't be measured. How the process happens remains a mystery, yet we can become conscious of what we think and how those thoughts affect us.

If you remain unconscious of your thoughts, then you're at the mercy of forces that Rick calls "magnetic tracks in the mind." When you become aware of thoughts that keep you stuck or cause you anxiety, you can interrupt them and alleviate your distress. Consider how relieved you'll feel when you can catch your samskara in the middle of a sentence and respond, "Here I am, worried again that I'll mess up." Doing so automatically makes you pause and take a breath, which interrupts the thought, giving you a moment to regroup and a chance to change your course. Later in this chapter you'll learn to substitute empowering thoughts that form healthy grooves in your mind, such as *Here I am. I can breathe and focus, and do my best.* Not only do you then create healthy tracks in your mind, but you also let the old ones that cause so much pain become dormant.

Lee's Story

Lee came to Mary's counseling office a year after separating from his wife of twenty years. Upset and confused, he knew he needed to finalize the divorce but worried that perhaps he shouldn't give up, that maybe the marriage could work out.

Over the next few months, Lee became aware of what fueled his anxiety. A dreamer, even as a child he wished for a brighter future. As a young boy he prayed that the next Christmas would be better, that his next birthday would be happier. The hope that maybe someday home life would improve had kept him going for as long as he could remember. He imagined a happy future as a way of coping with unhappy circumstances.

As he talked, Lee became conscious of a powerful samskara that had influenced him for over forty years. The samskara was the belief, *Home life is unhappy, and maybe it will get better.* Unconsciously, the samskara caused him to stay in a very unnurturing relationship. It was familiar for him to be unhappy at home and wish for things to get better. As he saw into the story, he felt great kindness for himself, both as a young boy and a mature man.

Recognizing the old story helped to release the hold it had on him and empowered him to relate more directly to the reality of the empty marriage he'd been in. He unhooked himself from the subconscious wish for a better tomorrow and became consciously interested in being happy in his present life. He finalized the divorce and began taking better care of himself. And when he caught himself wishing for a happier tomorrow, he paused, took a deep breath, and said, "I'm discovering how to enjoy my present life."

Be gentle as you approach your samskaras. If you tend to be critical of yourself, samskaras can become *something else that's wrong with me*, and you may use them as weapons against yourself. Beating up on yourself doesn't alleviate anxiety. Everyone has samskaric tendencies. Even though your suffering is personal to you, your samskaras aren't unique, and you're not alone in your tendencies. For now, when you hear the same old thing, take a breath and whisper to yourself, "Samskara—old innocent misunderstanding."

Becoming Aware

To become aware of samskaras, first we need to understand what we mean by becoming aware. Being aware means to take in information, to discern, or to be alert. Awareness doesn't produce experience; it notices experience. Neutral and quiet, without commenting, awareness simply shows you what's going on. Becoming aware of samskaras empowers you, because once something registers in your consciousness, you respond to it differently, such as when you discover a rut in the road and slow down or drive around it. In a similar manner, being able to soothe anxiety and find comfort in your physical body depends on your becoming aware of what's going on.

During an episode of heightened anxiety, your awareness focuses on the discomfort you feel. You're wrapped up in an experience of worry and fear, and don't know that you're unconsciously creating it yourself. All it takes, though, is something else to redirect your attention, and worrisome thoughts cease. For example, let's say you're nervous about something, and then the doorbell rings, diverting your attention. You walk to the door and greet your neighbor. You engage in brief conversation about the neighborhood picnic and, for a few minutes, have no anxiety. After the neighbor leaves, your attention reverts back to your concern, and you again experience anxiety. This example shows you that when you become aware of something other than your worrisome thoughts, your anxiety ceases. You don't have to wait for something else to interrupt your worry; you can become aware of what you're thinking and interrupt it yourself by directing your awareness to something soothing, such as your breath; a kind thought like *Hush, my dear*; or noticing colors in the room around you.

The Capacity to Direct Awareness

You can learn to direct your awareness. For example, you direct awareness away from thoughts and into action when you say to yourself, "Enough worrying; pay attention to doing the dishes." You can move awareness from thoughts to sensations to emotions. You can move it from inside you to outside of you, from a narrow to a wide horizon, and from grosser to more subtle stimulation. The easiest way to understand this is to experience it firsthand.

PRACTICE: DIRECT YOUR AWARENESS

1. For the first practice, you'll learn to direct your awareness up and then down your physical body. Take your time as you do this practice. Start by noticing your sit bones pressing down, and feel the sensation of your hips on the chair. Now move your awareness to your mouth. Notice your moist, soft tongue. Now direct your awareness to the back side of your neck and then slowly move your awareness

down your body, from your shoulders through your lower back, descending down into your hips and legs, and stopping with your feet. Feel the place where your feet touch the floor.

2. For the second practice, you'll direct your awareness from the periphery of your skin to the center of your body. Begin by being aware of the sensations in your fingertips. Now direct your awareness into your belly. Notice what you feel inside your belly.

3. For the third practice, you'll direct your awareness away from your body out to the area around you. Look at the colors. Notice primary colors, blends, shades, and the slight variations of colors. Notice the colors that are nearby and those that are farther away.

4. For the final practice, you'll direct your awareness to more subtle sensations inside yourself. Notice energy pulsating in your body, especially in your fingertips. Observe your breath flowing in and out of your nostrils. Be aware of the beating of your heart.

Helping Yourself

You can use the capacity to move awareness to help yourself. Knowing that worry doesn't relieve you, when you discover that you're worrying, move your focus elsewhere. Give your worried mind a break by letting your thoughts be without paying attention to them. Put some space between your attention and your worrisome thoughts. Tune in to the world around you. Use your senses: listen, see, smell, taste, and touch. Become conscious of what's happening around you. This literally brings you to your senses and makes you aware of life in the present moment.

If you feel the traces of anxiety or the pull of samskaras trying to take you back into distress, choose to focus on something pleasing. Listen to a song, look at a tree, smell the fresh air, drink a glass of water, or massage your forearms. Do something to refresh and restore yourself, and then go on about your day or address whatever you need to face.

become aware of what soothes and calms

Your awareness gravitates toward strong stimulation, which is why you notice loud sounds more than quiet ones. Imagine that you have a dove cooing on one shoulder and a parrot squawking on the other. You'll have a hard time focusing on the sound of the dove, because its cooing is drowned out by the higher pitch and volume of the parrot. You end up reacting to the parrot, and the soothing coos of the dove go unnoticed. In your mind, fearful thoughts are as loud as a squawking parrot, and soothing thoughts are often as quiet as a cooing dove.

It's difficult to dislodge your awareness from strong stimulation, whether it's a parrot or fearful thoughts. A parrot doesn't stop screeching just because you aren't paying attention to it, and neither do loud, fearful thoughts. Anxiety can be highly stimulating, and attempting to divert your attention away from it by focusing on soothing thoughts or something comforting in your environment may be ineffective at times. Next we provide interventions for moderate and intense distress. Both interventions involve moving your physical body or doing something that feels good to your physical body. They consist of shifting your awareness from mental and emotional pain to physical pleasure, which, of course, you can only be aware of as it occurs in the present moment.

Move Your Physical Body to Dislodge Awareness from Distress

If you're moderately agitated, it may take moderate stimulation to divert your attention. You may have to do something active, such as take a warm shower, walk the dog, or dance to your favorite music. If you have less time or aren't at home, find something else to take your attention off your anxiety. Go to the bathroom and wash your face; say, "Ahhhhh, ahhhh," loudly a couple of times; stand up and stretch; or walk over to a window and look outdoors. You don't have to suffer endlessly, but you do have to know what to do to help yourself and then actually do it. Even a thirty-second break can make a huge difference.

Sometimes strong distress requires an equally strong diversion. When you're absolutely beside yourself, try rigorously moving your body. It may snap you out of an anxiety trance or bounce you up out of a deep samskaric groove. But whatever you do, be aware of what you're doing so that it's not mindless activity. In chapter 6 we show you specific yoga poses you can do as a practice to relieve anxiety. For now we'll teach a movement intervention to shake awareness loose from anxiety.

PRACTICE: RIGOROUS SHAKING MOVEMENT

1. Stand up and stretch your arms over your head. With your arms overhead, sway from side to side to loosen up your body.

2. Now, bring your arms back to your sides. Take a big breath and begin to shake your hands—literally! Shake your hands rapidly; now shake your arms, and now your shoulders.

3. Next wag your hips from side to side. Lift your right leg and shake it, and now your left leg. Shake your feet, one at a time.

4. Now with both feet on the floor, shake your entire body for fifteen seconds.

5. Pause and stand quietly, and then rock from side to side. Now stand quietly, and notice the beating of your heart and the movement of your breath.

This simple movement requires no specialized training or athletic ability. It's strongly stimulating and captures your attention. It moves your awareness out of your thinking and into your body. Repetitive thoughts subside, and your mind quiets, allowing you to access common sense and to orient yourself to the present moment. Take another big breath and enjoy feeling relieved.

Alternatively, if you know the "Hokey Pokey" tune and dance, do that. We guarantee it'll pull you up out of a samskaric rut. We so love it that we've practiced this little jig with thousands of people.

PRACTICE: IDENTIFY AND IMPRINT MILD SOOTHERS

Identify what soothes you. Think of calming, pleasing things you do absentmindedly that would relieve stress if done intentionally. These activities can be as innocent as taking off your shoes and rubbing your feet, grooming your cat, or running your fingers through your hair; or as obvious as riding your bike or preparing a cup of hot tea. Identify your soothers now, while you're calm. List at least three. Write them down on sticky notes and stick them on your bathroom mirror. Practice them when you're not upset. Practice them for the simple sake of enjoying them and as an intentional practice. Practice each one daily for a week to imprint your soothers through repetition. Then, when you catch yourself worrying, your soothers will come to mind, and you'll know what to do to help yourself.

Choose Health and Happiness

Anxiety is an unpleasant experience. Whatever you do to redirect your awareness or soothe yourself, aim for a pleasant experience that's good for your health and happiness. Consider the effects of your behavior. Laughing with a friend, skipping around the house, and splashing your face with warm water are all healthy and feel good.

Eating a dozen cookies, drinking a bottle of wine, and shopping for clothes may initially feel pleasant, but have unhealthy aftereffects. True pleasure soothes and has a lingering residual. It doesn't cause mental or physical distress an hour later or the next morning. It relieves pain and contributes to your well-being.

Awareness and Sensitivity

Samskaric worries, trauma memories, and old stories cause you to be highly internally stimulated, anxious, and unable to relax. If this becomes a chronic state, you're perpetually overloaded, which is numbing and weakens your capacity to enjoy simplicity, subtlety, and beauty. Your ability to enjoy living is diminished to the extent that a simple meal and quiet evening don't satisfy you. It may seem as if you need more stimulation, but unfortunately, more doesn't soothe. Flurry and excess as a lifestyle don't alleviate anxiety; they exacerbate it, because they numb you to the point where you can't read your body's stress and fatigue signals. Since you're unable to pick up subtle cues, your body is at risk of developing more serious symptoms.

You also become unaware of what's nearby and precious, such as the gift of life that comes in each breath, the faithful beating of your heart, and the wisdom of inner guidance. Used to being bombarded by activity and noise, you may become uncomfortable with silence, which is a great loss since silence is incredibly peaceful. It also connects us with the eternal, as is stated so clearly in Psalm

46:10: "Be still and know that I am God." Frenzy doesn't alleviate anxiety, but quiet does, because in stillness, there's no anxiety.

A mantra also alleviates anxiety. It takes you inward, into your inner quiet places, where you can connect with peace and your eternal self. Using a mantra is a truly wonderful way to begin becoming comfortable with less stimulation, because it focuses the mind on a thought or sound that's comforting and lets you slowly unwind your need for activity.

the practice of mantra

A *mantra* is something you repeat to yourself over and over. You fill your mind with the sound of a word or phrase that touches you deeply. It's a form of attentional training in that you recite your word again and again until it's wired into your brain and forms a life-affirming samskara. Reciting your mantra can be so soothing that, after a few minutes, you simply become quiet and enjoy stillness. The word "mantra" means a sacred thought or a prayer. It can be as simple as a single syllable, such as "Om"; a number of syllables, such as "Shalom"; or two or more words, such as "Thy will." In *The Heart of Yoga*, T. K. V. Desikachar (1999, xix) tells us that rather than being a Hindu symbol, the mantra is something much more universal that can take our minds "to a higher plane." He goes on to explain that every spiritual tradition has its sacred words.

We recommend that you select a mantra that you love and feel deeply connected to. Many people choose a mantra from the tradition closest to them and in their own native language. If you're a Christian, you may prefer calling it "breath prayer" rather than mantra, and you may want to select a short prayer or Bible verse to recite. However, for a variety of personal reasons, you may prefer to search for your mantra outside of the tradition you were raised in. While there's no one word that's the perfect mantra, there's probably a word or phrase that compels you at this time in your life. Mantras have powerful influence. You've undoubtedly been captivated by the words of a powerful orator. You not only heard the words but also felt them. The words moved you, perhaps even motivated you to take some action or make some change. So that you can be moved, select a mantra that has a strong, positive effect on you.

PRACTICE: DISCOVER YOUR MANTRA

Choose a word or phrase, possibly from your spiritual tradition, that touches you deeply. Feel its effect on you. Select a mantra that has a calming, reassuring, or empowering effect on you.

Your mantra might be the name of a spiritual figure, such as Jesus, God, Allah, or Buddha. You may prefer a word or phrase that conveys a spiritual quality, such as "Shalom," "Be here now," "Mercy," "Let go," or "Trust." You may want to express gratitude with the mantra, "Thank you." Or you may choose to recite words such as "Amen," "Om," **So-ham** (Sanskrit for "I am that"), or "I am." You may gravitate toward a phrase from a spiritual song; a line from a sacred poem; or perhaps some scripture, such as "I am with you always" or "Be still and know." Mary's current favorite mantra is "Stay here, my dear, stay here," and Rick's is "Live with ease."

We've described a variety of words and phrases to inspire you. Now it's your turn. Select a mantra. You may want to try out a few to discover which one resonates most deeply with you.

Once you have a mantra, you're ready to spend time with it and form an intimate relationship with it. You do so by repeating it. A mantra is powerless unless you practice it. You can recite it mentally or say it out loud. How you speak to yourself makes a huge impact on you. When you recite your mantra, whether you speak out loud or say it silently in your mind, use a calm, kind voice.

What you say to yourself has tremendous ramifications, so why not say words and utter sounds that elevate your level of consciousness? Rather than deepen an anxiety samskara by reciting the same worrisome thought a thousand more times, practice reciting your mantra. Fill your mind with words that infuse you with compassion and strength, or that remind you that you're a conscious or spiritual being.

When you're anxious, your breathing is more shallow and rapid. Therefore, it's helpful to recite your mantra on your outbreath. This slows down your breathing, which relaxes you and allows the mantra to permeate more deeply. Discover it for yourself.

PRACTICE: USING A MANTRA ON THE OUTBREATH

Use the mantra, "Relax."

1. Give yourself one minute for this practice. For the next sixty seconds, simply say the word "relax" silently on each outbreath.

2. Notice how your mind quiets and your body tension eases.

PRACTICE: EXPRESSING GRATITUDE

Use the mantra, "Thank you."

1. Give yourself another minute. Simply say the phrase, "Thank you," on each outbreath.

2. Notice that your energy feels softer and warmer. Let yourself enjoy the experience.

When you're anxious and stuck in an old samskara, you may forget to practice your mantra. So, let your mantra practice you. Write your mantra on several sticky notes. Post your mantra notes in different locations, including one on your bathroom mirror, one beside your bed, and one on your refrigerator. Your computer, phone, and desk are great places also. When you see your mantra on a sticky note, smile to yourself, and then recite and enjoy your mantra.

Nicole's Mantra

One day Nicole, a counseling client, said to Mary, "I need a mantra; my old supervisor has come back." His return had triggered Nicole's post-traumatic stress disorder. She had painful memories of working for him previously, and feared that he would misuse his power again. His loud voice and authoritarian ways reminded her of her ex-husband, who had physically abused her. A shy woman, Nicole had lived alone since getting out of her marriage, and felt isolated. She benefited from support but had very little. After some thought, Mary offered this mantra, a scripture from Nicole's religious tradition: "I will not forsake thee."

Nicole said it out loud a few times, and then responded, "It's not quite right." She paused, flushed, and whispered, "I know my mantra: 'he will not forsake me'!" Then she smiled at the idea of being supported by the divine. They recited the mantra together a few times, and Nicole began to cry softly. Mary handed Nicole a sticky notepad, and Nicole wrote her mantra on seven notes. She told Mary where she would post them, that one would go on the dashboard of her car so she would see it on her drive to work, and one would go in her lunch pail as a noontime reminder.

They role-played various conversations with Nicole's supervisor. Nicole practiced mentally saying her mantra during the conversations. The focus calmed her. Afterward she reported, "I didn't fall into my victim thinking during the role-playing."

Mary instructed Nicole to say her mantra out loud when reminded by the sticky notes. Reading, speaking, and listening to her mantra would embed it deeply in her body and mind. Mary knew that if Nicole didn't practice her mantra when calm, she would forget to say it to herself when stressed, especially during interactions with her supervisor. During her next session, Nicole reported, "My mantra is working. I whisper, 'He is with me' under my breath when my supervisor comes into my area, and I don't freak out nearly so much."

the practice of taking the opposite point of view (pratipaksa)

Pratipaksa is a practice you can use to limit the damage of negative, scary, destructive self-talk that arises from old stories and trauma. The practice, from *Yoga Sutras of Patanjali*, as interpreted by Mukunda Stiles in 2002, is a method for assuming another, opposing, point of view. This is another practice that helps you forge healthier patterns in your brain and allows old samskaric patterns to become dormant, like unused trails in the woods. According to the Yoga tradition, there are two kinds of thoughts: *Klishta* are helpful thoughts that encourage and align you with reality, such as *I can breathe and take it one step at a time. Aklishta* are injurious thoughts that discourage, distort, and predetermine your experience, such as *Just forget it; I'll never get this done.*

Practicing pratipaksa requires becoming aware of the thoughts that cause you the most pain. The way you determine how your thoughts affect you is by noticing how you react to them emotionally and physically. Self-critical, pessimistic, and worrisome thoughts are injurious, and cause your body to tense or tremble and your mood to become distressed.

Let's put this to practice. When you hear a self-critical thought, pause. Stop, and then step out of the old tracks by taking a breath and responding, "I deserve kindness." Replace pessimistic thoughts with an encouraging thought, such as, *Life is as it is; good things also happen.* Substitute worrisome thoughts with *Stay here, in the present moment.*

Pratipaksa is not for engaging in a battle between opposites. Responding to *I'm stupid* with *I'm smart*, or *I'm ugly* with *I'm beautiful* may result in an "am too, am not" argument. Engaging in endless debate doesn't end pain. The intent of pratipaksa is to heal and correct, not to perpetuate suffering. When substituting the opposite word helps you, this is true pratipaksa. You can tell if a word is helpful by your reaction to it; you don't have to believe it, but it should, at least, be one that you don't recoil from. One way to keep from running away from healthy words and actually create space for them is to take a couple of breaths and repeat the words, giving them a little time to etch into your mind. This begins rewiring your brain with life-enhancing words.

To work with pratipaksa, identify particular thoughts that hold you back. Detect devastating thoughts, the ones that beat you down, such as: *I'll never trust again, My life is ruined,* or *I'm really messed up.* These thoughts paralyze you, convince you that you're no good, and prevent you from knowing your innate preciousness. Replace destructive thoughts with life-affirming ones, such as: *Trust this moment, this breath; It's okay; Stay right here; I made a mistake;* or *I'm sorry, I didn't know.* These thoughts give you breathing room and touch your heart with kindness. They reassure you of your basic worthiness.

Also look for the frequently occurring thoughts that drag you down, such as: *Oh well, it doesn't really matter; Just put it off until later;* or *I can't do it anyway.* These thoughts, heard over and over, erode your sense of worth and capacity. They're hindrances that prevent you from fulfilling your potential. Life-enhancing thoughts include the following: *Trust what your heart wants; Just begin; Take one step; Yes, my dear, yes, you can.* A best friend talks to you this way, so talk to yourself as if you're your best friend. Encourage yourself. Don't settle for the negative voice; implant an empowering voice. Doing so not only feels good but propels you forward, moment by moment, into the wonderful potentiality that you have.

PRACTICE: PRATIPAKSA

Write down a thought that's most devastating and then a thought that just drags you down. Come up with a thought to counter each. Make your response a thought that appeals to you, that has a soothing and corrective effect. Write the thought at least seven times to embed it and remember it. Sing the thought. Put it to a melody. Make it playful if you like, because little songs play over and over in our minds.

Rick's Pratipaksa

Rick had a drag-you-down thought that went like this: *There must be something wrong.* It seemed he could only allow so much happiness, because after things went smoothly for some time, he would start to worry. One day he sang his negative thought to the melody of "The Farmer in the Dell." His song went like this: "There must be something wrong / There must be something wrong / Hi-ho the derry-o, there must be something wrong." Then some days later, he added another verse: "There's really nothing wrong / There's really nothing wrong / Hi-ho the derry-o, there's really nothing wrong!" Now when he starts to wonder if something is the matter, he sings his song as loud as he can. After a round or two, he laughs and goes on about his day, relieved and back on track.

the practice of determination and resolve (sankalpa)

Anxiety samskaras rob your focus, zap your energy, and deflate your determination. If you're like us, there have been times you've

119

known you needed to do something yet didn't do it and turned away from your deepest desires out of fear. Most likely, what was missing was sufficient internal backing and fortitude, because with enough support and focus, you can move into your potential and away from anxiety-driven living. *Sankalpa*, or yogic goal setting, supplies the sustenance you need.

In *Path of Fire and Light*, volume 2, Swami Rama (1986) stresses that with sankalpa, you create powerful, new positive samskaras. When you focus on new samskaras, the old ones become inert. You don't have to remain stuck or repeat old habits; you literally have the capacity to recreate your life and focus on what's important and dear now. With sankalpa you garner the courage, one-pointed focus, and determination needed to do so.

Sankalpas are goals on the level of thought. You repeat the thoughts daily, and they imprint the mind forcefully. The desired thoughts then become activators, generating decisions and actions. Then surprisingly, you find that you follow through with whatever it is you truly want.

The following is a sankalpa format we learned during a retreat with yoga teacher Rod Stryker.

PRACTICE: CREATE A SANKALPA

To create a sankalpa, use the following guidelines.

1. Develop a specific goal to achieve over the next few months or the coming year.

2. State a resolution. The first half of the sentence is a daily resolution. It's an action you do daily to bring the desired quality into your life. The second half of the sentence is a tangible result that occurs over time.

3. As you select and write your resolution and result, do so with great appreciation. Truly, your sankalpa empowers you

to transform your life, and that's a lot to be thankful for. It's a treasure, something to appreciate.

4. Write your sankalpa according to this format:

    I resolve to _____ daily so that the result is _____.

Following is a list of sankalpas to illustrate how to develop them:

- I resolve to do yoga stretches for ten minutes daily so that the result is experiencing ease in my physical body.

- I resolve to witness my thoughts for fifteen minutes daily so that the result is seeing my thoughts for what they are, phenomena of the mind.

- I resolve to work in my yard for twenty minutes daily so that the result is having a beautiful flower garden.

- I resolve to write for twenty minutes daily so that the result is writing a book of my memoirs.

- I resolve to talk with a friend daily so that the result is having a supportive social network.

Remember, what you think about, focus on, and put energy into takes form in outer life. Write three or more sankalpas. Dare to write your truest dreams and take yourself seriously. Honor your needs and let your heart express itself.

PRACTICE: PRACTICE YOUR SANKALPA

Now, select your most important sankalpa. Write it on a separate piece of paper. Speak it out loud and listen to yourself say it. Feel your sankalpa and picture yourself doing it. Place your written sankalpa by your bed. Read it just before you go to sleep every night to allow it to make a strong indentation in your mind.

Tell your sankalpa to somebody you trust, as a way of sharing your heart and your intention, and energizing your sankalpa. Show yourself that you're serious about your sankalpa by being accountable to another living being. Select a trusted person to telephone weekly and report about your sankalpa. If your friend also has a sankalpa, you can be sankalpa buddies and check in with each other weekly. If you don't have a friend to share with, speak the sankalpa out loud several times a day.

You may work with more than one sankalpa. If you wrote a couple that feel really important and timely, take them both in as your sankalpas. You know yourself and how you operate. If you have difficulty with discipline or follow-through, begin with one.

No matter what, keep imprinting your sankalpa into your mind. The most important act is reading it every night before you go to bed. Enjoy reading it and make it your friend. Follow through with your daily resolution as best you can, yet understand that you're human and you may slip. Practice every day you can, even if only for a few seconds, and give thanks on the days when you do. And over time, enjoy the accumulative results of the sankalpa.

the practice of stillness

Perhaps the simplest and most profound practice for deactivating old patterns is taking time to be still and quiet. Sitting down and doing nothing gives you a chance to unwind and let your mind relax. You literally stop moving long enough to get your bearings, to see where you are and what's going on. You know what it's like when you can't take it anymore and you want the world to slow down. You've probably even said something like, "Stop this train and let me off." Well, you can get off the samskaric train by taking time for stillness.

This daily process of being in silence and stillness can be comfortable rather than burdensome. If you drink coffee or tea in the morning, find a comfortable chair to sit in, possibly one with a view of the outdoors, and sit quietly and enjoy your beverage. If you usually have the television, radio, or music on when you're home, turn it off for a half hour. Gradually increase your time in silence so that it feels comforting. As you make friends with silence in your home, you'll experience the same profound stillness that arises up in you when you're at a quiet temple or a beautiful park.

Eventually, stillness becomes a refuge where you connect with yourself in places that aren't influenced by your old tendencies. If you haven't already, you may discover a still place within. The closer you come to this inner stillness, the more it fills your body and mind with peace. You have a conditioned self and an eternal self. Silence connects you to your eternal self and is deeply therapeutic.

The following two practices facilitate your deepening intimacy with silence.

PRACTICE: NOTICE STILLNESS

1. Stillness is in the space between breaths. For a few breaths, notice the stillness before and after the outbreath.

2. Stillness is in the space between thoughts. Pause, notice the stillness in the gap between thoughts.

3. Stillness is in the gap between words. Enjoy the stillness between the words on this page.

4. Tune in to stillness in your room. Sense stillness in your body tissues.

5. Listen and notice stillness.

Plan a time to go outdoors to befriend stillness. Take a slow stroll in an attractive, safe park or neighborhood. Enjoy walking, and notice stillness all around you. The sun and the grass are quiet. So are park benches, traffic signs, and butterflies. Take pleasure in discovering stillness.

PRACTICE: EXPLORE THE EFFECTS OF SILENCE

Notice that silence expands. Feel how it calms. Relax and breathe. If you experience boredom or fear, direct your awareness to your soft belly. If you notice thinking, recognize it as thoughts, perhaps about boredom or fear, creating discomfort. Silence itself is comforting. Whisper, "This is a thought," and smile knowingly.

How Silence Heals

Silence heals. Let's liken your life to a beautiful pond. Anxiety keeps you stirred up, like a relentless wind blowing across the water. When water is being continually whipped, you can't see its depths. When you relax into silence, your restless winds die down and you can see into your inner essence. If a difficult memory arises, you witness it, say, "This is a memory; it's not happening now," and focus on breathing in and out to reconnect to the present moment and detach from the image or thought in your mind.

When you become comfortable with silence, your capacity increases to truly look at yourself and at life. It's as if you see from a place deep inside. Rather than observe from the old perceptual distortions, you look out from deep within. When you're highly anxious, you look through the eyes of fear. You see danger where there is none, but once you become rooted in silence, you look from silence. Seeing is more objective, neutral. Amazingly, this process begins to heal deep fears. Fear of being alone or in the dark begins to dissolve. When you don't look out through the eyes of fear, these deep fears aren't reinforced.

PRACTICE: ENJOY SILENCE

For a moment, pause, breathe, and take pleasure in outer silence. Notice that the book is quiet, the chair is quiet, and the walls are silent. Listen to silence and relax into it.

The Practice of Retreating

If you want to accelerate your healing and deepen your ability to be comfortable in your own skin, plan to take a retreat. Taking time away from your ordinary life is a powerful way to step away from the momentum of samskaric imprints on your mind, rest your exhausted body, and connect with your inner guidance. Retreat is a prearranged break from work, daily routines, and casual social contact. A time for personal space, it allows you to focus on your practices, reflect on your life, and simply rest and be in silence. Following a retreat schedule creates a break from daily patterns and helps you to see the ways in which you live mechanically.

Having time away allows you to see how you create anxiety and to make new choices that enhance your health. You may discover a painful belief, such as *There's nobody there for me*, and substitute a life-enhancing belief, such as *I have all the help I need*, and then write a long list of all the help that's available to you and how you can ask for and receive it. You may discover that you're exhausted and have to take long naps while retreating, and then develop a sankalpa that says, "I resolve to nap for thirty minutes over my lunch hour daily so that the result is having better physical well-being."

While you don't need to go to a retreat center to retreat, most of them are located in spacious, tranquil settings surrounded by wilderness. Their beautiful, quiet environments feel safe and are conducive to retreating. So if you choose to plan a retreat, whether at a center, at your home, or in a cabin by a lake or woods, make it a setting that feels like a safe haven.

Retreats can be so therapeutic that we want to give you a sense of what it's like to go on one. To invite inner silence, formal retreats involve sustained periods of social silence, meaning there's no small talk or gossip. There may be teaching sessions guided by the retreat leaders, with focused discussions, journal writing, or both, but beyond that, there's generally no talking.

How long you retreat is up to you. If you've never taken time to retreat, try a day or a weekend. The major retreat centers offer retreats that last anywhere from a weekend to several months. You can retreat at home alone or with a group at an organized retreat. Since both have advantages, we recommend a bit of both.

Retreating at Home

Retreating at home is inexpensive because there are no travel, lodging, or registration fees. You can arrange the retreat according to your convenience and start small if you prefer, scheduling the length of your first retreat from a half day to a weekend. This way, you gradually get used to giving yourself a little time and space.

Prepare for it in advance. Tell family and friends that you're planning a retreat and that, for its duration, you won't be available to talk in person or by phone, except in case of emergency. Let them know that you'll check your phone for important messages. If you're married or have a close friend, consider doing the retreat together. If you have children, make fun arrangements for them. Knowing that they're enjoying themselves helps you to relax into your retreat. If your partner is uninterested in retreating, simply plan the home retreat when your partner is gone, or rent a cabin at a retreat center, state park, or wilderness area. Whatever you do, make it easy and accessible.

Design a retreat schedule. Write it down and post it somewhere noticeable so you can follow it. Make your retreat agenda inviting and restful. If you're exhausted, plan on a later wake-up time. On the following page is a sample retreat schedule for a one-day retreat.

Retreat is for resting your body and mind, nurturing yourself, taking a breather away from your life, and connecting with your inner self. Therefore, if you retreat at home, do so in a way that's pleasing. Make it soothing and enjoyable. Retreat is not for deep housecleaning or major yard and garden projects. It's not for academic or fiction reading, or catching up on bookkeeping, correspondence, or to-do lists. In other words, it's not for working.

Retreating with a Group in an Organized Retreat

Attending an organized retreat has advantages as well. You stay at a retreat center away from home, which eliminates the temptation to do house, lawn, and computer work. Your basic needs are tended to, including meals, so you can rest and be with yourself.

You have the benefit of having one or more retreat leaders, who offer guidance, present teachings, and lead individual or group processes that focus your retreat experience. Another advantage of retreating with a group is support and structure. Knowing that you're not alone makes it easier to follow the schedule and honor silence. The group creates a compassionate energy that sustains participants and makes your inner exploration safe and transformative.

Sample Retreat Schedule for Home

7:00 a.m.	Wake up.
7:30–8:00 a.m.	Do gentle yoga stretches and breathing exercises.
8:00–8:30 a.m.	Do seated meditation.
8:30–9:30 a.m.	Have breakfast, do cleanup, and lounge a bit.
9:30–10:30 a.m.	Hike, walk, or if tired, rest.
10:30–11:30 a.m.	Read in sacred book and reflect in personal journal.
11:30–noon	Do seated meditation.
noon–2:30 p.m.	Have lunch and take free time for napping, writing poetry, drawing, painting, and doing nothing.
2:30–3:30 p.m.	Do outdoor or indoor mindfulness meditation (sit or stroll comfortably in a quiet place of beauty and enjoy the sights and sounds around you).
3:30–5:30 p.m.	Write a prayer or gratitude list, or a message from your heart to yourself; massage your hands and feet; and so on. Enjoy your free time, have tea and a healthy snack, and prepare dinner.
5:30–6:00 p.m.	Do seated meditation.
6:00–7:30 p.m.	Have dinner, do cleanup, take relaxation break; stroll outdoors, sit on the deck, and so on.
7:30–8:30 p.m.	Write in a journal about your retreat experience or share it with your retreat partner.
8:30–9:00 p.m.	Do evening meditation.
9:00 p.m.	Prepare for bed.

conclusion

All experience arises in the present moment. Your thoughts and old samskaras create a lot of what you experience. Repetitive thoughts and behaviors create grooves in your subconscious that perpetuate old ways of thinking and living. Fortunately, you can stop this cycle and become aware of what's happening. You can also learn to soothe yourself when your experience is stressful, and form life-enhancing habits.

You can rewire your habitual nature by implanting wise and loving thoughts through pratipaksa, mantra, and sankalpa. You can also befriend silence and discover its presence in yourself, for stillness is the source of profound healing and great happiness.

It's important to heal both your body and mind. A comfortable body makes for a quiet mind and an open, joyful life. To help you be relaxed and happy, next we move into yoga poses and breathing practices.

chapter 6

practices for comforting your body

Your life becomes a temple of that which is sacred when you choose to live with love in this moment.

—Swami Chetanananda

It's next to impossible to be aware of the presence of the sacred when your heart is closed off, and anxiety and trauma make you want to shut down at times, disconnect from your loving nature. Your healing depends on your opening up again and remaining open. It's also difficult to experience your life as holy when your body is tight, ever bracing against possible danger. Whether or not you're aware of it, anxiety takes a toll on your body and your heart. One of the safest, most effective ways to open your heart and comfort your body is with a regular, gentle practice of yoga poses.

Once your body and your breath have been saturated with fear, they mutually reinforce your distress and perpetuate anxiety. Because of their close relationship, when you practice yoga poses, it's important to also focus on your breathing. You stretch, move, and hold poses while being aware of your breath. The alchemy of doing so makes your practice transformational and more than just physical exercise. Fortunately, you don't have to be physically fit to practice and benefit from yoga for anxiety.

A wisely selected practice of enjoyable yoga poses that are within your physical capacity helps clear the effects of anxiety out of your body and heart, especially if you practice them on a regular basis. Taking ten to fifteen minutes daily to do a few poses keeps your body free of stored-up anxiety in the same way that regular brushing keeps your teeth and gums free of bacteria. The poses we teach in the following pages are safe, feel good, and restore a sense of comfort to your body. The poses are for use as necessary, for those times when you're overwhelmed or need extra comfort. We teach five easy poses you can do daily, and we've added five additional poses you can take into your daily practice when you have time for a longer practice. Then we conclude with a couple of yogic breathing practices because learning to breathe fully is so therapeutic.

How you practice these yoga poses depends on the kind of person you are and how you experience anxiety. To help you select a way to practice that really suits you, here's a little information about what other people have discovered. John Kabat-Zinn, founder of the Stress Reduction Clinic at the University of Massachusetts Medical School, and colleagues (Kabat-Zinn, Chapman, and Salmon 1997) found that people who experience anxiety more as mental distress tend to like to move and strengthen their bodies in their practice, and those who feel anxiety more as distress in the body prefer a quieter, less physical, meditative approach. So, if you're a worrier, you may want begin your practice with poses that heat your body, such as the bridge-pose flow (where you move into and out of the pose several times), or the muscle-strengthening poses, such as boat and staff, for a while and then gradually add advanced variations of poses to your practice. If your body feels trembly and you're upset, try a gentle practice, such as the five easy poses; do a couple of minutes of alternate nostril breathing; and then sit in meditation. All of these poses and breathing techniques are introduced later in this chapter.

Judith Lasater (1995), a specialist in restorative yoga, found that during times of exhaustion, people benefit most from supported poses that they rest in for several minutes. In these poses you prop up your body with blankets, pillows, and yoga blocks (yoga props approximately the size of two thick books) so that you feel supported and don't strain. Restorative poses feel safe and emotionally stabilizing while gently allowing your body to open and relax. If you're fatigued from recent or ongoing trauma, the restorative pose for emotional fatigue (introduced later in the chapter) may be therapeutic for you and may be the only pose you practice until you feel up to doing the five easy poses.

Doing yoga poses to reduce anxiety makes good sense. They're relaxing, relieve muscular tension, and strengthen muscles. However, the benefits extend far beyond the physical. They give you a basic sense of having a solid foundation, help you to assimilate your experiences, and empower you to live with an open heart. To explain these underlying benefits, let's look at energy centers.

psychoenergetic centers (chakras)

In the same way that powerful currents travel through the ocean, energy continuously moves through your body and mind. Although energy travels in many directions in our bodies, a particularly strong current moves along the spine. There are also energy centers, called *chakras*, along the spine. Three are below the heart, and three are above it.

Energy can become trapped within these centers. One way to get a sense of trapped energy is to compare it to muscular tension. Muscles are designed to contract when needed and relax when not being used. When muscles are tense, they remain contracted, which you experience as spasms, stiffness, and discomfort. When your muscles relax, you feel comfortable in your body. Similarly, trapped energy in your chakra centers impacts you dramatically. Perhaps most obvious is what happens when your heart chakra is closed off, which causes you to feel cold hearted, indifferent, or even untouched by suffering and joy. When your heart chakra is open, you feel friendly, receptive, and warm.

Like water flowing down the Mississippi River into the Gulf of Mexico, it's optimal to have energy flowing freely throughout your body. Anxiety disrupts this flow by causing tension and agitation. The three chakras that most directly pertain to anxiety are the root support (muladhara), jewel fortress (manipura), and unstruck (anahata). Yoga poses for anxiety focus on these three energy centers.

Root Support (Muladhara) Chakra

The first and lowest chakra, muladhara, is located at the base of the spine at the perineal floor. The Sanskrit word *muladhara* means "root support." This center reflects basic survival issues.

According to Gary Kraftsow in *Yoga for Transformation* (2002), this chakra relates to your hips, knees, and feet. Located at the base of the spine, this chakra represents stability. As you well know, when you and your life are stable, you're more apt to feel safer and find it easier to trust, and when things are unstable, you may feel more fearful and mistrusting.

Trauma pertains to survival, because it disturbs your sense of safety. Energetically stored in the lowest chakra, trauma causes tension in the hips. Initially, when going through a rough time, you naturally tighten and protect yourself. But to stay closed is unfortunate. There comes a time to open, to be receptive to life again; otherwise you're immobilized and disempowered.

Yoga poses that release stored tension in the hips are therapeutic for anxiety, because they unlock and relax the body tissue around the hip area. Forward-folding poses, such as what you do when you sit down and bend over to tie your shoes, are effective at releasing tension from your hips. If you stay in forward-folding poses for a while and focus on taking slow, steady breaths into the areas where you feel the stretch, the energy that traps fear is released from your muscles.

Jewel Fortress (Manipura) Chakra

The third chakra is located in the navel region. Its name, *manipura*, means "jewel fortress" and poetically points to the underlying truth that you are a jewel. This chakra corresponds to self-worth and self-image, which we all know is easily distorted, in that we forget who we are. Because this is so important, we repeat it again. You're precious beyond measure; experiences don't alter your essence. When you remember this, you digest life experiences more easily, and when you don't, you can have blockage in this chakra, which leads to low self-esteem and difficulty accepting change.

There are two kinds of poses that work on your belly area, or core. Poses that strengthen your tummy muscles and reinforce

135

this chakra are beneficial if your anxiety comes from a feeling or notion that you simply can't deal with life. The resulting sense of strength shatters your belief that you can't cope. Equally important are twisting poses, where you rotate your spine first in one direction and then the other, as you do when you twist around and look behind you before you back your car out of a parking space. Twisting moves energy through the area of your gut. This helps you to "digest" experiences, much as you do food, assimilating what you can and moving on out what you can't. If you work with this chakra, the resulting sense of resilience is a great antidote for anxiety caused by unprocessed experiences.

Unstruck (Anahata) Chakra

Fourth is the anahata chakra, located at the base of the sternum, close to your heart. *Anahata* means "the unstruck sound." This chakra relates to the heart, lungs, spleen, and thoracic spine, and reflects emotional issues. Constriction in this chakra can show up as insecurity, nervousness, anxiety, and an overly critical nature. Opening this chakra unlocks your courage to follow your inner guidance, and restores your willingness to take emotional risks with others and feel fully alive as a human being.

Since fear can cause you to close your heart, it's vital to compassionately keep your heart open, because a closed heart robs you of the happiness that comes from loving. Back-bending poses open and lift your chest, similar to what you do when you step outdoors to look at the night sky, put your hands on your hips, and tilt your head back to see the stars directly overhead. Back-bending poses, which stretch back your shoulders and expose your heart, release grief and make space for new life. Gentle back-bending poses are therapeutic for the anxiety caused by any belief or experience that has convinced you that you can't love or be loved.

qualities of the physical practice of yoga

How you practice the poses is as important as which poses you do. Next are two styles of practice that have very different results. Depending on how you carry anxiety and what's going on in your current life, you may find one of these approaches more useful in reducing anxiety.

Purifying and Cooling

Since anxiety revs up your body and speeds up your breath, yoga poses for anxiety generally focus on cooling the body and slowing down your breath. Therefore it's helpful to move slowly, breathe comfortably, and gradually allow your body to relax as you go through your poses. Consider how refreshing an afternoon nap is or how rejuvenating it is to rest midway while hiking up a mountain. Both of these activities calm and restore you. In yoga, purifying techniques include gradually lengthening the outbreath, briefly pausing after exhaling, closing your eyes during poses, practicing restorative forward bends, doing inversions (or upside-down poses), and doing some seated or supine spinal twists. They reduce agitation and tension in the body, and slow down the breath.

Expanding and Warming

At times heat and effort are needed to melt tension. Long-trapped tension may need to be met with equal force in order to be released. You've probably experienced being so stressed that you had to go outdoors and jog or do some physically demanding task. You simply had to use up all the pent-up energy.

In yoga, expanding techniques include keeping your eyes open during poses, moving quickly, and doing standing poses that build endurance and vigorous poses that are energizing, such as back bends. If you carry a lot of muscular tension, you may benefit from beginning your practice with poses that require strength and endurance. After heating the muscles, which thaws tension, you can then relax into more calming yoga poses.

Breathing and the Poses

Whatever form of practicing the poses you prefer, remember to breathe. Many people say that what they most carry from yoga class into their daily lives is the ability to take deep breaths and to focus on breathing when they're stressed. If you do the yoga postures without paying attention to your breath, you only get partial benefits. In fact, it might be helpful to make a sign that says, "Breathe," and prop it up in front of you to help you stay aware of your breathing while doing your poses.

Props and the Poses

We recommend trying the poses in this chapter before investing in props to use with your poses. You can easily substitute common household items for formal props. Using props can greatly enhance the quality of your experience as you do yoga poses. Typically, yoga props consist of a yoga mat, a strap, a block, and a yoga blanket, and for restorative yoga, add a bolster. However, you need none to do these yoga for anxiety poses. A long, supple belt or a man's tie works well for a strap. A thick telephone book or folded bath towel works well for a block. You can use a large beach towel in place of a yoga mat, and a couple of pillows will work as a bolster. Before you begin your daily asana practice, have your props or alternatives close by so you don't have to interrupt your practice to find them. Then, as your commitment grows, you may want to purchase a yoga mat and other items.

YOGA POSES TO REDUCE STRESS

Stress reduction poses purify your body as they release tension and soothe trembling. Let's begin with a "minibreak" pose, something you've instinctively done countless times. A great time-out even though it's not a formal yoga pose, it's relieving and can be done almost anywhere. It's very comforting to take the weight of the world off your mind by holding your head with your hands and closing your eyes. In **Yoga as Medicine** (2007, 12) Timothy McCall gives these instructions: "Gently move the flesh between your eyebrows in the direction of your nose." Try it and you'll discover that it's relaxing to gently tug your eyebrows down.

Minibreak Pose

Sit facing a table or desk. Place both of your feet on the floor. Put your hands on your forehead, with your fingers holding your head and your palms on your eyebrows. Put both of your elbows, shoulder distance apart, on the table or desk. Close your eyes. Gently press down on your head with your fingers and move your eyebrows slightly down toward your checks. Place your awareness on your breath and rest in this position for several breaths.

Minirest Pose

Place your forearms on the table and rest your forehead on your arms in "minirest" pose. Gently press your eyebrows down toward your cheeks. Focus on breathing in and out for several rounds.

Forward-Folding Poses

Because they're so calming, forward folds are great stress reducers. Poses of introversion, they feel safe because you curl your body into itself. Your belly and heart are protected. They also stretch the hips, release the muscles of your lower back, and open the first chakra area. Here are two tension-reducing forward folds you can do at home, in your company's break room, or in your office.

Buttocks-Against-Wall Forward Fold

Loosen your belt and clothing around the waist and neck. Take off your shoes. Stand by a wall, facing the center of the room, with your feet hip-width apart, six to eighteen inches away from the wall. Press your buttocks against the wall. Bend your knees and let your head hang toward the floor. Rest your hands on the floor, or hold your ankles or legs with your hands. Alternatively, position a chair in front of you, and place your hands on the chair. Focus on breathing for six to ten breaths. Feel your spine elongate, and your hip and back muscles relax.

Seated Forward Fold

Make sure your clothing is loose around your waist and throat. Sit comfortably on a chair and bring your feet and knees hip-width apart. Lean forward, resting your chest on your lap and your hands on the floor. If your chest doesn't reach your lap, hug a pillow or two between your lap and chest. Be aware of breathing. Stay for six to ten breaths. Feel the comfort of the pose.

YOGA POSES THAT COMFORT

These next three poses are very calming. Use them when you feel upset or overwhelmed. They have a purifying effect, and are ways to be kind to yourself.

Comfort Pose to Reduce Emotional Upset

Lie on your back with your knees bent and your feet on the floor, or a sofa or bed. Place one hand over your heart and one on your tummy. Move your hands until you find the spots that feel just right. Pat gently on your tummy to draw your attention to the area. Now pat or rub your heart to draw your awareness to the heart area. Notice the surface you're lying on; feel where your back presses down into it. Feel the sensations of your hands on your body. Breathe easily and fully while resting in this pose, and stay in it until you feel soothed.

If you like, transition into the next pose. It softens your muscles around your spine, stretches muscles around your hips, and releases tension from your lower-back muscles.

Restorative Pose for Emotional Fatigue

Restorative pose for emotional fatigue, also known as "supported, supine bound-angle," not only feels safe and supportive but also focuses on the first and third chakras, gently opening your hips and muscles around your heart area. You need a bolster and three blankets. (One or two sofa pillows and three beach towels work well.) Place a folded blanket at one end of the bolster. Lie down on the bolster, resting your head on the blanket and your buttocks on the floor. Touch the soles of your feet together, separate your knees, and place a folded blanket under each knee. Rest your hands, palms up, beside your body. Adjust your blankets for your comfort. Close your eyes. Rest and relax. Remain in this pose for several minutes. Focus on the rhythm of your breath or recite your mantra.

Nurturing, or Happy Baby, Pose

This pose is a gentle hip opener and, as such, focuses on the area of the first chakra. Lie on your back. Bend your knees up toward your chest. Wrap your arms around your legs and hug them into your chest. Stay there and allow the lower back to become accustomed to the position. Move your knees away from your chest, toward your underarms. Clasp your big toes with your first two fingers and thumbs. Alternatively, wrap your arms around the back sides of your thighs, or position a strap around your thighs and hold the strap with your hands. Soften into the pose. Remain there for several minutes and pay attention to your breathing. If it's comforting, gradually lengthen your exhalations for a few breaths.

HEATING-YOGA FLOW

If you feel tense and need to engage heat to melt away persistent muscular tension, try doing a warm-up series using the bridge-preparation pose. You do the bridge pose with your hands at your sides, and the bridge-preparation pose with your hands overhead.

Bridge-Pose Flow

Lie on your back with your arms down at your sides, bend your knees, and place your feet hip-width apart on the floor, about six inches away from your hips. Keep your knees over your feet. On inhalation, press down on your feet, tuck your chin down toward your chest, and lift your hips up, forming a smooth bridge from shoulders to knees. Lift your hands over your head. On exhalation, return to the starting position. Bring your hands down beside your body. Repeat these two poses.

Coordinate your movements with your breath. Lift up your hips when you breathe in, and bring them back down when you breathe out. When you lift, start with your hips and move up vertebrae by vertebrae. When you come down, unwind the spine, from the upper back down. Do this sequence for six or more times, until your muscles are warmed and you feel less tense.

Now you're ready for the five easy poses.

A DAILY YOGA PRACTICE FOR ANXIETY: THE FIVE EASY POSES

The following practice calms body and mind. While these five easy poses are helpful for relieving a particular episode of anxiety, they're designed to be a foundation for a daily practice. If you're new to yoga, these are great poses to begin with. They feel good, and you don't have to be physically fit to begin working with them. They take less than fifteen minutes, so they don't require a large time commitment. However, you do have to practice them in order to receive the benefits. If you can't do some of the poses, simply skip them. Focus on the other poses rather than try to force your body to do something it can't do.

These five poses are relatively easy for most healthy bodies.

Easy Pose 1: Bridge Pose

Lie on your back, with your hands extended beside your hips and your palms facing up. Bend your knees and place your feet about six inches away from your hips. Keep your feet and knees hip-width apart. Inhale and lift your hips up. Pull your shoulders close together. Either let your hands stay resting on the floor, or clasp your hands together. Press on your shoulders and lift your chest. Hold the pose for six to twelve breaths. Feel the effort in your buttocks and thighs. Gently attempt to move your heart toward your chin and allow your chest to open. Come down and rest for a few breaths, and then hug your knees to your chest.

Easy Pose 2: Upward-Stretched Legs

Keep your arms by your sides. Raise your legs up in the air and stay for a few breaths. Then extend your arms overhead, if it's comfortable; otherwise leave them at your sides. If it's uncomfortable to straighten your legs, bend your knees or place a block under your sacrum. Once you're in a comfortable position, focus on the in-and-out movement of your breath. Hold the pose for six to twelve breaths. Come down and hug your knees to your chest.

Easy Pose 3: Staff Pose

Sit erect and tall. Put your hands behind your hips to support the lengthening of your spine and opening of your chest. Tuck your chin toward your chest and look down. Stay there, or if you can, stretch your arms overhead and bring your chin up so you can look straight ahead. Focus on breathing in and out. Hold for six to twelve breaths.

Easy Pose 4: Bound-Angle Pose

Sit with your spine erect. Bring the soles of your feet together, comfortably close to your groin. Place your hands behind your hips to support the lifting of your spine. Bow your chin toward your chest. Stay there for several breaths.

If it's comfortable to do so, clasp your feet with your hands. Bring your chin to a neutral position, and either look at the floor a few feet in front of you or close your eyes. Focus on breathing in and out for six to twelve breaths.

Easy Pose 5: Child's Pose

Begin on your hands and knees. Place your knees a little wider than hip-width apart. Lengthen your buttocks back toward your hips, and lower your chest toward your thighs. Rest your arms overhead or at your sides. Place a folded blanket under your head for support, if desired. Allow your forehead to rest on the blanket or floor. If this is uncomfortable for your knees, roll up a blanket and place it on your lower legs, close to your knees, for support. Stay there for eight or more breaths. Relax and enjoy.

This concludes the five easy poses practice. This is a great ten-to-fifteen-minute practice, which may be enough for you, especially in the beginning. As you desire, you can lengthen your practice by simply repeating the five easy poses.

A DAILY PRACTICE: THE EASY POSES PLUS FIVE ADDITIONAL POSES

To advance your practice gradually, begin adding additional poses to the easy poses, as outlined next, for a total of ten poses. A modified sequence of the easy poses follows, beginning with bridge pose, with instructions added for the additional poses.

Easy Pose 1: Bridge Pose

Hold for six breaths.

Easy Pose 2: Upward-Stretched Legs

Place a block under your sacrum for more inversion.

Additional Pose 1: Modified Supine Pigeon

Lie on your back and bend your knees. Place your feet on the floor. Lift your left leg and cross your left ankle over your right thigh. Bring your right knee halfway toward your chest, and clasp both hands around your right thigh. If your hands don't quite reach around your thigh, place a strap around your right thigh and clasp both hands to your strap. Draw your right knee into your chest and gently push your left knee away. Feel a stretch in your left hip. If you're comfortable, stay there. Otherwise, deepen the stretch by extending your right leg. Clasp your leg or foot with your hands or a strap. Stay there and focus on your breath for six to twelve breaths. Focus on gradually lengthening your outbreath. Switch sides. Repeat the pose on the second side.

Easy Pose 3: Staff Pose

Additional Pose 2: Boat Pose

Begin in staff pose. Bend your knees and lift your legs in the air. Or, if your abdominal muscles are weak, keep your toes on the floor. Balance on your hips. Extend your arms beside your legs or hold your thighs with your hands, if needed. Stay there and keep your knees bent, or extend your legs with your knees together. Breathe deeply for six or more full breaths.

Additional Pose 3: Spinal Twist

Begin in staff pose. Bend your right knee and place your foot beside your left knee. Lift your spine to make yourself tall, and place your right hand approximately one and a half feet behind your right hip, fingers pointing away from your body. Keep your spine long and straight as you lean back. Place your left elbow on your right thigh. Rotate your spine to the right side.

As you inhale, lengthen your spine, and as you exhale, gently rotate. Stay in this pose for at least twelve slow breaths. Enjoy the sensations.

Change sides and repeat this pose, rotating your spine to the left. Hold the pose for a minimum of twelve relaxed breaths.

Easy Pose 4: Bound-Angle Pose

Stay in the pose for eight to twelve long, even breaths.

Additional Pose 4: Head-to-Knee Pose

Begin in staff pose. Bring your left foot to your right thigh, and place the sole of your foot on your inner thigh. Rest your right leg on the floor. Bend your right knee unless you have flexible hip and leg muscles. Raise your arms overhead to lengthen your spine, and then lean forward with your chest and lower your hands to clasp your thigh, lower leg, or foot. Breathe and feel the stretch. Stay in this pose for eight to twelve rhythmic breaths and slowly extend your right leg as your body permits. Enjoy the pose. Switch sides. Bring your right foot to your left thigh and repeat the pose on the second side.

You may put a folded blanket across the extended leg to rest your forehead on, or place a block under the bent leg to support your thigh and knee.

Easy Pose 2 (Repeated and Modified):
Legs-Up-Wall Pose (Upward-Stretched Legs)

Place one or two folded blankets about six inches away from the wall. Sit close to the wall, with your right side facing the wall, buttocks positioned next to the blanket. Roll onto your back, with your sacrum resting on the blankets. Lift your legs up and rest them on the wall. Make yourself comfortable. Relax and enjoy. Stay in this pose for a minimum of fifteen breaths.

Additional Pose 5: Corpse Pose

Lie on your back. Bend your knees and flatten your lower back onto the floor. Extend your legs out on the floor, hip-width apart. Reach your arms out and down, palms in the air. Let your back relax and your body melt into the floor. Be comfortable. If needed, place a rolled blanket under your knees to relieve lower-back tension, and place a folded blanket under your head to relieve shoulder or neck tightness. Take a few conscious deep breaths. Scan your body from head to feet. Be aware of being in your body. Follow the rising and falling of your breath. Enjoy stillness and let go into relaxation. Stay there for five to ten minutes.

BREATHING PRACTICES

After completing your physical yoga practice, you'll likely feel refreshed. This is a wonderful time to do a brief breathing practice. It just takes a few minutes, and the rewards are many. If you find that focusing on your breath causes discomfort, rest for a minute. Stay in your comfort zone.

Breath or Energy (Prana)

Prana is a word with many meanings. Most simply, it means "breath or respiration," but it also means "life," "vitality," "wind," "energy," or "strength." The words are all interrelated because you have to have breath in order to live. Yoga offers breathing practices to help you attain healthy breathing. You already know that the breath of anxiety tends to be shallow and rapid. Ideally, our breath is slow and full, which you can reinstate by lengthening your exhalations and gradually deepening your inhalations.

You can literally recondition your breathing so that you breathe fully more of the time. Spend some time working with your breath, and gradually you'll be inclined to breathe that way even when you aren't attending to your breath. Begin by becoming aware of your breathing as it is. Then do a few rounds of the following practice.

Breath Retention

Breath retention is a method of retraining the way you breathe. In this practice, you inhale, intentionally retain your breath, and then exhale. To make it easy and smooth, coordinate your breathing by mentally counting. Breathe in as you count to four. Retain your breath for the count of two, and then breathe out as you count to four. Do this for a few rounds until your breath gradually deepens. Then breathe in for the count of six, retain your breath as you count to three, and breathe out as you count to six. Do this for a few breaths, as long as you're relaxed. Then, release your efforts, and simply sit and enjoy being aware of the pleasant sensations of breathing for a few breaths.

This is a gentle practice, so please don't force. At the first sign of distress, let go of the practice and relax all efforts. This is not intended to increase tension. The goal is slow and rhythmic breathing, and decreased tension.

Alternate-Nostril Breathing

Whether or not you're aware of your nasal cycle, you have one. Your breath alternates between your right nostril and left nostril throughout the day and night. Check for yourself. Close off your left nostril, and breathe in and out through your right nostril. Now close off your right nostril, and breathe in and out through your left nostril. You probably notice that you're breathing in more through one nostril than the other.

Right-nostril breathing is warming and energizing. Left-nostril breathing is cooling and restorative. Predominately breathing through the right nostril triggers the sympathetic nervous system's fight-or-flight response, and predominately breathing through the left nostril triggers the parasympathetic system's relaxation response. The yogic practice of alternate-nostril breathing is believed to balance the sympathetic and parasympathetic nervous systems as well as your overall energy. This is a gentle practice. If you find it stressful, take a rest.

Take a comfortable seated position. Bring your right hand close to your nose. Gently close your right nostril with your thumb, and inhale through your left nostril. Release your thumb, lightly cover your left nostril with your last two fingers, and exhale through your right nostril. Now inhale through your right nostril. Release your last two fingers, cover your right nostril with your thumb, and exhale through your left nostril. This is one cycle of breathing. Repeat a few cycles. Notice the calming effect.

Cooling Penetration

Here's a breathing practice to do when you're stressed or tense. It's a great mini–stress break. Since the breath of anxiety is predominately right-nostril breathing, you can stimulate the relaxation response by breathing exclusively in through your left nostril and out through your right nostril for a few rounds. Then resume normal breathing, and be aware of the movement of your breath. Enjoy the simple act of breathing.

conclusion

You can use yoga poses individually, as needed, to relieve distress, or group them together as a daily practice to gradually open and relax your body, restore your ability to love, and develop personal strength. Doing a carefully selected practice in less than fifteen minutes not only soothes your body but also increases the flow of energy through your body. To maximize the benefits of your practice, focus on your breath while holding the poses, which increases your ability to concentrate, puts your attention in your body, and brings you into present-moment awareness. Add a few minutes at the end of your session to recondition your breath. Over time the benefits of a daily practice accrue as your body releases accumulated stress and relaxes. A healthy body not only feels wonderful but also quiets the mind and enables you to focus on what really matters to you.

chapter 7

meditation and mindfulness for anxiety

Centering prayer, a meditative method, is a seeking of a true relationship with God or the Ultimate Reality. Take time each day to be with yourself, out of respect for yourself. In this tumultuous, noisy, and active world, you need to be in touch with your deeper self, beyond the ordinary psychological awareness that preoccupies you.

—Father Thomas Keating

meditation is taking some quiet time to sit; focus your attention on your breath, mantra, or stillness; and witness your thoughts. When you catch yourself thinking, you simply put your attention back on your breath, mantra, or the silence in or around you. After a while, thoughts subside, at least for a moment or two, and when that happens, you feel peaceful. Any anxiety you feel begins to fade. If you meditate as a spiritual practice, as Father Thomas Keating teaches, then those quiet moments are a time to connect to higher consciousness.

Meditation trains you to become more conscious of what's happening in your body and mind, and teaches you to be aware of life in the present moment. Meditation helps you to witness and identify thought patterns that contribute to anxiety, and because meditation orients you to the present moment, it nourishes and comforts you as only being in the now can do. So that you can observe your mind and avoid getting lost in the past or future, meditation practices give your attention something to focus on. And, in the moments when your mind is quiet, you're aware of stillness, and experience inner peace.

withdrawal of the senses

One way to focus your attention is by paying attention to only one of the senses. A simple way to experience this is to shut your eyes and press your thumbs against the openings of your ears, closing off your hearing. Hum gently and listen to the sound of your humming. This simple exercise focuses your awareness on what you hear. Doing so narrows your attention and withdraws your engagement from the world around you. Since we take in information from the outer world through our sensory capacities, withdrawing your senses means to retreat from active, multiple-sensory inputs. The restriction can be to one sensory input, such as gazing at a lit candle, or you can retreat from all sensory inputs. You would begin classical yoga meditation by taking refuge from sights, sounds, smells, and activities. This is why instructions to meditate begin with sitting in a quiet, still place.

Lying awake in bed at night is similar to meditating with your eyes closed. During the night, the world around you is quiet and still, taking rest. The room is dark, and the surrounding environment recedes from your awareness. You experience withdrawal of the senses, yet you can still have all kinds of experiences. Your mind may generate thoughts, emotions can arise, and you may have bodily sensations, but then a few minutes later, you might lie there awake, contented and peaceful. While both meditating and resting in bed are times of little sensory input, they have different goals. As you lie in bed, your purpose is sleep and nonawareness, whereas when you sit for meditation, your intent is to be awake and aware.

When You're Sleepy

You may feel sleepy during meditation since sleep is highly associated with sensory withdrawal. Don't be discouraged if this occurs, because it may indicate that you need more sleep. See what happens when you simply witness the sleepiness. You may discover something interesting about yourself, and if you doze off, it's no big deal. Sooner or later you wake up again. Another option is to meditate with your eyes open, gazing softly at the floor or some object, since open eyes are associated with alertness.

concentration

When you concentrate, you direct your attention to something specific. Like a laser beam, you home in, aiming to stay focused. Concentration involves intention, and is the opposite of drifting or distracted attention. The yogis of the East taught that a preliminary stage of meditation is teaching the mind to be fully engrossed in a single focus. Developing the capacity to concentrate takes some practice, but the benefits are well worth the effort, because concentration calms your restless mind, which is great medicine for the worried mind that jumps hither and yon.

You prepare for concentration by sitting in a quiet room. Absence of external stimulation makes it easier to train your mind to become one pointed. The next step is to give your attention something to focus on. Breath and mantra are two great choices for concentration. Breathing is essential to life, and mantra aligns you with higher consciousness. Experiment with both to find which is more appealing. Most likely you'll gravitate toward one. Go with what works naturally for you. Make your practice enjoyable so that you don't want to skip out on it.

Concentration consists of focusing, discovering when you're not focusing, and returning to your desired focus. Having something to concentrate on is like having an anchor to the present moment. When you realize you've drifted off into thoughts, put your awareness back on whatever you're focusing on, and once again, you'll be alert and aware. It's like saying, "Oops, I drifted away, and here I am again."

Focusing on the Breath

The breath is wonderful to focus on, because putting your attention on breathing tends to slow it down, which triggers the relaxation response. Also, as long as you live, you breathe, so breath is readily available. You can pay attention anytime you like. Focusing on the breath as you meditate trains you to be more aware of your breathing in general, which has two effects: your breath evens out, becoming more rhythmic, and you find yourself being aware of your breathing off and on throughout your day. You literally begin to experience your breath as an intimate friend, always there.

There's no one way to attune your awareness to your breath. Experiment to find a way to become aware of your breath that feels right for you. One suggestion is that if you're new to meditation, you may find it comforting to focus your attention on the movement of air going in and out of your nostrils. The nostrils are a distinct and specific area to focus on. The nostril openings are at the surface of the skin and focusing on that area can feel safe if you're uncomfortable tuning in to sensations inside your body.

You may also focus your awareness on the breath in your chest area, inside your body. Put your attention on the movement of your ribs. Feel them expand as breath comes in, and contract as breath goes out. Another way is to focus exclusively on your abdomen. Feel it rise and fall in response to your breath. The belly area is larger and less distinct than the nostrils, and involves a diffuse, soft focus. Alternatively, you may find it appealing to follow the breath's entire journey as it travels in and out of your body.

Focusing on a Mantra

Focusing on a mantra is equally wonderful. When you fill your mind with the words and sounds of higher consciousness, you align yourself with wisdom, love, and peace, which soothes your body and mind, and expands your perspective. Silently repeat your preferred word for the divine, such as the Hebrew word *abba*, meaning "father," or use a word that represents some spiritual quality, such as "mercy."

Reciting a mantra while meditating cultivates concentration, and plants the mantra in your consciousness, where it takes on a life of its own. It begins to recite itself, in the same way that lyrics to a song you heard on the radio replay in your mind. If you say your mantra daily in meditation, it will plant itself in your mind with deep roots. Then, it's with you, like a true friend, giving you the steady support you so need when you're nervous.

Some people find it uncomfortable and anxiety provoking to focus on the breath during meditation. If that's true for you, select a mantra as your focal point. If you're anxious, experiment with saying your mantra on the outbreath. Doing so tends to lengthen your exhalations, which triggers the relaxation response.

Focusing on Stillness

After you've acquired some experience meditating, experiment with focusing on stillness. It's quite lovely, and can lead to a deep inner state of peace and quiet that Father Thomas Keating described, while teaching during a retreat, as "sitting in the lap of God." You may want to begin by focusing on your mantra or breath until your mental activity subsides, and then switch and pay attention to silence. Notice the silence outside of you, in the room you're in, and inside of you, in the space between thoughts. Allow yourself to become absorbed in stillness. Doing this gradually helps you to become comfortable with silence so that over time, you'll grow to love it.

When Attention Drifts

Attention does drift, especially back to your thoughts, which is perfectly normal. Thoughts are stimulating and are used to having your attention. Attention is a creature of habit, and does what's familiar. As you sense the power of the pull back into thinking, you realize how untrained your attention is. In meditation even nonevocative, mundane thoughts snare your attention, which helps you appreciate the difficulty of disengaging from highly evocative, scary thoughts.

During meditation, when you notice that you're paying attention to thoughts, calmly redirect your attention back to your breath or mantra. It doesn't matter how many times you have to do this; it matters that you do it. Each time you refocus, you strengthen your concentration.

witness your thoughts and refocus

While meditating you do nothing with your thoughts other than let them be. After all, when your mind generates thoughts, it's just doing what it does. Your task is to gently refocus your awareness on your breath, your mantra, or the stillness. Let your thoughts remain without paying attention to them. Doing so has two effects: One is a sense of space between you and your thoughts. The other is subtle yet noticeable: focusing your attention settles your mind. It becomes quiet and contented as you sit there. You may find that even your mantra or breath awareness recedes into stillness as you go into a deeper meditative state of peacefulness.

Techniques for witnessing your thoughts can be helpful. A popular one is to let your thoughts pass by like clouds in the sky. Comparing thoughts to clouds offers great perspective. In that same way that a cloud mass may be large but doesn't fill the entire sky, your thoughts can't cover your entire consciousness. They seem to do so, because they're "loud," persistent, and demanding. Yet they don't. As soon as you witness your mind activity, you're no longer immersed in it.

Witnessing Your Thoughts Is Nonviolent

Concentrating on your breath, your mantra, or silence is like coming home to a peaceful place. Return to your focus after discovering that you're engrossed in thoughts, and then, from the comfort of your home, look out at thoughts as they pass by as if they were billowing clouds drifting along in the sky. The entire process is utterly nonviolent. There's no need to pressure or scold yourself. Gentle persistence is the way. Let's look at why.

You learn by observing. If you watch an expert chef make piecrust, you'll learn the secrets of making great crusts, such as how to transfer the rolled crust to a pie pan. Witnessing your thoughts while meditating yields knowledge about them, as long as you're a benevolent witness. Approach a chef with hostility, and he's less likely to show you how to make pies. In the same manner, your mind reveals its fears, misunderstandings, and deepest desires to you when conditions are safe. Ridicule what your mind shares, and it may retreat. Above all, witnessing is kind. Quietly, respectfully listen, and over time, you'll likely hear your inner secrets, such as why you're afraid of the dark and what you truly yearn for.

Your thinking mind responds to compassionate witnessing. Sometimes it becomes quiet and rests as you watch over it. Other times it shows its contents to you: how it repeats thoughts, what it worries about, and whatever else it wants you to know.

Witnessing Your Thoughts Is Relational

Witnessing is an allowing, or permissive, relationship with your thinking mind. You let thoughts go by, and at the same time, you see them. It's like sitting by a stream and watching the leaves float by. You're attentive yet noninterfering. If you begin stirring up the leaves, you muddy the water and lose your capacity to see clearly. If you worry about where they're going, you become anxious. When you simply sit and watch, you relax and may well discover something about how leaves journey through water.

You've probably told a tender story to someone who truly listened. You felt heard, somehow seen by that person. Talking to someone who gives you attention is healing. When you witness

your thoughts, you give this quality of attention to your thoughts.
As the witness, you step aside to see what the mind does. Rather
than identify with your thoughts, you have enough distance from
them to learn about them. In doing so, you see yourself.

Witnessing Your Thoughts Creates Internal Space

Developing the capacity to witness soothes the turbulence of
your inner life. You're less rattled by emotional ups and downs,
because in addition to, reacting emotionally, you watch yourself
react. The same thing occurs with your editorial mental mono-
logue. You observe what you're saying as you say it, which creates
internal space between witnessing and thinking. Then, after meditation, as you go about your day, you can see your comments as
thoughts, which gives you some space to decide how you want to
respond to them, or if you need to respond at all. Many thoughts
are like wisps of clouds in the sky that are insignificant and require
no response at all.

how to meditate

Select a quiet and peaceful place to meditate. Place a chair or meditation cushion in your spot. Designate a time of day for meditation
so you can practice at the same time each day. Early morning is
often recommended as a good time to meditate, but any time that
fits your lifestyle and appeals to you will work.

Once you have a time and location for meditation, commit to
practicing daily. Even if you have only a few minutes, take time
for meditation each day. Make meditation really approachable in
the beginning. Start small; sit for five or ten minutes. This makes
your meditation practice friendly and achievable. Then over time,

gradually build up your sitting time from fifteen to thirty minutes, or longer.

PRACTICE: BASIC MEDITATION INSTRUCTIONS

1. Sit comfortably with your spine upright.

2. Set a timer for a designated time, from five to thirty minutes.

3. Give your attention something to focus on, such as breathing or a mantra.

4. Release your effort to quiet the mind. If you find yourself drifting off in thought, just return your attention again and again to your breath or mantra.

Meditation is actually quite simple, so relax and begin to explore it. Meditation can seem a little intimidating, and you may become concerned that you're not doing it right. But in all truthfulness, as long as you go to your meditation spot daily and put your awareness on either your breath or your mantra, you'll benefit.

Learning to Meditate During Times of Stress

Anxiety can challenge your ability to concentrate and drain your willpower. While meditation is great medicine during times of distress, it can be challenging to practice at such times, especially if you're a novice meditator. So be gentle with yourself, sit for brief periods, and remember that this is a nonviolent practice. Berating yourself for not focusing well is not effective. Kindness and persistence are required to coax a fatigued attention span into focusing.

Make your meditation practice simple and nurturing. Begin by reading a couple of sentences, or a short phrase from a sacred text or devotional book. Nourish yourself with words of wisdom and hope. Sit for a few minutes and digest what you read. Then, when you're ready, set your timer for five to ten minutes, and meditate.

Meditating Relieves Anxiety

When you suffer from anxiety, meditation can be your life-line. Although you may initially flounder a little with how to do it, once you're comfortable with meditation, you'll return to it daily. It becomes a sanctuary, a place of refuge. You gladly go to your chair or meditation cushion, because you know its benefits.

At the very least, meditation is a relief from busyness. You're taking time to be with yourself. While meditating, you usually sit in a quiet room to give yourself a break from overstimulation and overactivity. As such, it's relieving, even though your mind occasionally generates thoughts. On noisy-mind days, focus on your breath or your mantra, watch what your mind is doing, and enjoy the moments when there's less mind chatter. While some meditation sessions are more enjoyable than others, none are worthless. On the days when your mind is less active, enjoy your peaceful state.

After you've obtained some experience meditating, you can access inner stillness, even if only for a moment. Here's how it happens: You begin your practice the way you usually do, by focusing on your breath or reciting your mantra, and then all becomes quiet. For as long as it lasts, you connect with stillness. The next thing you realize is that your mind tosses out a few thoughts and recaptures your attention. The moments and minutes when you fall into deep quiet are fortunate, because in that quiet space, anxiety dissolves, and you feel incredible peace.

Meditating on Your Heart

When you need tender support, focus on your heart chakra. In *The Heart of Meditation*, Swami Durgananda (2002, 220) says that the heart center is "where the inhalation comes to rest...beneath the breastbone, four to five inches below the collarbone." In this meditation, focus on the breath flowing in and out of your heart center. Swami Durgananda instructs you to even "enter the space inside the heart center. Let the inner space of the heart expand with the breathing, softening and widening" (128). You may sit with your hands in a prayer pose, place your right hand over your heart, or fold your hands on your lap. Do what's comfortable and natural. If you like, breathe kindness into and out of your heart. Feel the radiant warmth of your heart. Connect with the compassion you feel. Let yourself be held in the embrace of your heart. This is a wonderful meditation for comforting yourself.

While doing a research project, our friend Hal read in *The Biology of Transcendence*, by Joseph Pearce (2002), that the cells of the heart muscle are 60 percent nerve cells (as in the brain), and in the first moments after conception, they exhibit life and movement. Miraculously, mysteriously, they take on a rhythm of their own, which they maintain until you die. After completing his research, Hal had heart surgery. Afterward he had a sense of being "disconnected" in ways he'd never before experienced. Knowing that his heart had been momentarily stopped during surgery and that a heart-lung machine had maintained his life, he wondered if he had lost touch with the greater source in the process.

During his recovery period, he did heart meditations and made a breakthrough discovery. While meditating he searched for the source of his heartbeat and held the image of connecting with that greater source. After several days of this meditation he had powerful experiences of oneness with the infinite. You may want to sense into the mystery of your heartbeat so that meditating on your heart also connects you with your original source.

mindfulness practice

You don't have to separate your meditation practice from your daily life. You can witness your thoughts and focus on your breath or mantra whenever you remember to. Practicing meditation in this way during the day is called "mindfulness practice." To make this clearer for you, let's define "mindfulness." A simple definition is "nonjudgmental acceptance of things as they arise in the present moment." It involves noticing what's happening inside and outside of you so you can see things as they are.

An easy example is relating to your worrisome thoughts mindfully, which is simply responding to them the same way you do when you meditate. When worry arises, witness it and place your attention on your breath. When you notice a thought like, *Oh no, what's going to happen?* recognize it as a thought and return your focus to your breath. Taking a breath is nourishing and reorients you to what you're doing and where you are. Breathing intentionally pops you out of your thought trance and provides immediate relief, because it puts some space between you and your fretting.

Mindfulness, or nonjudgmental witnessing, is a tall order because it entails getting in touch with what you experience moment to moment. You can only witness what you allow yourself to be aware of. As someone who's prone to anxiety, you have a natural tendency to want to detach or escape from it, and now you're being counseled to get in touch with it, to witness it.

Allowing What Is

Mindfulness involves accepting what is, and it's through this acceptance that anxiety is reduced. This acceptance includes thoughts, emotions, and physical sensations. It's impossible to accept what you don't allow yourself to be aware of. Let's apply this to anxiety. "Allow" signifies consenting to, letting it be, and giving yourself permission to feel anxious. We recognize that you don't want to feel anxious and that you're probably whispering, "Why would I want to feel anxious?" The answer is that doing so empowers you to breathe through your anxiety so that your resistance doesn't intensify it or cause you to be paralyzed by it. Here's how it works.

Focusing on breathing steadies you so that you don't get lost in worry or overwhelmed by anxiety. Leaning on your breath allows you to witness anxiety. Anxiety may be intense, but you don't get swept away by it when you remember to breathe. Your breath is your constant companion; let it steady you so that you can focus and observe your anxiety. Learn about anxiety in a precise way: how long it lasts, its level of intensity, what escalates it, and what calms it down. When you take the mystery out of anxiety, it loses some of its hold on you, and when you discover that you can breathe through anxiety, you're less trapped in its spell.

Allowing is not related to passivity. It doesn't mean nonaction; in fact it's a precursor to empowered action. Without the ability to see clearly, there's no insight. If what you know is distorted or incomplete, your decisions are misinformed. The best choices arise out of accurate understanding. Therefore, let yourself see "what is." Allow whatever arises in your experience without distorting it.

A Great Question and Response

Stop, breathe, and ask, "What's going on now?" Pause, focus, and sense into your body. Notice sensations. Scan for tension and for nontension. Tune in to your emotions. Listen for thoughts. Register what's happening in your experience.

Smile gently and say, "I allow this experience." Notice any tendency to recoil. Smile at your aversion and say, "I allow even this."

Naming What Is

Give your internal experiences a name. Let's return to the earlier example of the thought, *Oh, no, what's going to happen?* Allow the thought so that you can be aware of it, and then focus on breathing in and out. Now name it: *This is a thought.* The act of naming has the effect of creating a little distance from the experience without suppressing it. You can also name emotions and sensations. When you're afraid, let yourself notice your tight muscles and racing heart. Breathe and name your experience. Say, "This is fear," and breathe again. Something helpful happens. You're still frightened but not totally encased in fear. Naming gives you a little room. Your breath becomes fuller. You experience "what is" without being confined in it.

Putting It All Together with Breath Awareness

Mindfulness puts you in touch with life, and focusing on breathing is the lifeline that enables you to do this. For that reason breath awareness is central to mindfulness. It puts you back in your body and gets you out of your thoughts. If you don't want to miss out on life, practice being aware of your breath coming in and going out.

You know what it's like to watch a movie and become distracted by worrying about tomorrow. You miss an entire conversation on the screen, and then refocus on the screen and try to figure out what's going on. You turn to your friend, who's also watching, and ask, "What did he say?" Your friend answers your question, and you both miss the ongoing conversation between the actors. Now two people are scrambling to catch up with the movie.

Now let's say that you watch the movie and practice mindfulness. Most of your attention is on what you see and hear on the screen, and a small part of your attention focuses on your breath's in-and-out movement. As a result, you're less likely to be taken away by your thoughts, but when you do, you more quickly realize it. Focusing on the continuous flow of breath keeps you observant, preventing you from becoming consumed by thinking. So not only do you suffer less from fretting about the next day, but you also avoid missing as much of the movie or diverting your friend's attention away from the screen.

Walking a Path of Mindfulness

A lovely form of mindfulness practice is walking meditation. In this meditation you walk slowly, take small steps, and coordinate your movement with your breath. Take a few steps on each inbreath and each outbreath. Let your breath be comfortable. Notice each foot as it steps. Feel where your feet touch the ground or floor. Pay attention to how your heel steps down, how your foot rolls, and how you push off from the front of your foot with each step. Paying attention like this helps you to be in the present moment rather than get ahead of yourself. Enjoy breathing and walking. Do this leisurely, slowly. Relax as you stroll.

Walk to walk! You're not hurrying to some destination, wandering mindlessly, or getting exercise. You're paying attention to your experience in the present moment while walking. When practicing outdoors, look around as you slowly walk. Feel the air movement and the temperature. Take in the sights and sounds while coordinating breath with movement. This trains you to be aware of what's happening in you and what's going on around you in the present moment. We love to walk in the woods and study the trees and leaves, touching bark, smelling vegetation, and watching the rays of sunlight flicker through the leaves. Another favorite is stepping outdoors on the deck and watching crows, hawks, and turkey buzzards fly overhead. Rick shows Mary the different flying techniques of the birds, and we stand transfixed for a moment, absorbed in the present moment. Sometimes we stroll over to the fishpond and watch the goldfish. When we go back inside to our home office, we feel refreshed and soothed. Mary occasionally mindfully walks to and from the restroom when she's working at her counseling office. You can practice mindful walking in any location, and it's beneficial to practice even for a few moments.

Practicing the walking meditation indoors is a great alternative to nervous pacing. Intentional focusing makes all the difference. Breathe out, take three small steps, and look at the floor. Breathe in, take three small steps, and notice colors. And on you go, observing and striding. Continue walking until you feel calm, which is how you'll know that you've engaged the relaxation response.

Implementing Mindfulness

Practicing all the elements of mindfulness—being aware of breathing, allowing, noticing, naming your inner experience, and taking in the details of your surroundings—results in your living in life's present, moment-to-moment unfolding. Of course, that's easier said than done! Fortunately you have endless opportunities to practice, and practicing is quite fun. Here's how you do it. When you brush your teeth, notice where your toothbrush is in your mouth, feel its pressure, taste the toothpaste, notice your saliva, and, of course, notice that you're breathing in and out. When thoughts arise, name them "thinking." When you feel rushed, name this experience "rushing." That's a lot to be conscious of!

In the beginning, practice mindfulness when you're doing enjoyable tasks to make it easy to stay in the experience. It doesn't matter if you practice while driving the car, drinking coffee, taking a shower, or walking around the block. What matters is that you practice. After some practice, experiment with tasks that you typically don't enjoy. You'll discover something very relieving: the task isn't as tedious or unpleasant as you thought it would be. You'll just do what you do, and who knows? Since you'll be calm, you might find more enjoyable ways to do what needs to be done.

conclusion

As simple as meditation and mindfulness are, these practices can be personally challenging. Approach these skills as if you were learning a new dance step, mastering a piece of music, or refining your table-tennis skills. Give yourself some time, and understand that your efforts are beneficial and don't depend on any certain experience in meditation. If your mind is busy, you're enhancing your ability to concentrate and witness. If your mind is quiet, you access inner quiet and calm. As Father Thomas Keating said to Mary, "God appreciates all efforts at friendship." We encourage you to keep your appointment with meditation. Give a little of yourself and your time to meditation, and it will give you much in return.

chapter 8

relieving anxiety with ethical living

One of the greatest duties we have in the world is to become the individual we were called to be.

—John O'Donohue

Something extraordinary happens when you live with openness, possibility, and compassion. You discover as you move through your day that you feel real, engage in life, and have the capacity to deal with anxiety as it arises. The teachings of yoga have given us principles to live by that are truly healing and can help us fulfill our destiny of finding real happiness and inner peace. As we practice, we discover our anxiety lessening moment by moment.

principles of self-restraint

The first set of principles shows us how to live harmoniously with others. They help us manage our primitive survival instincts that can easily go awry and cause many problems, including perpetuating trauma and chronic fear. We've transformed some of these principles into practices that can help you heal anxiety, prevent its recurrence, and live peacefully.

Nonviolence

First and foremost is the principle of nonviolence. Violence begets more violence. The effects of violence, aggression, and hostility live on in your body as the neurophysiological fear response. It lives on in your mind as thoughts of dislike, judgment, fear, revenge, and victimhood. Harboring violent images or exposing yourself to violence in movies triggers your body's stress response just as do real-life violent acts. Ongoing exposure to violence can desensitize you to its effects, causing great damage, including paralyzing anxiety. The practice of nonviolence begins with the pledge, "No more violence," which means to avoid voluntarily consuming violence for entertainment, or thinking, speaking, or acting in ways that perpetuate violence in your life.

194

When you truly love, you don't want to inflict pain. Unkindness is not an expression of love; its motivated by fear, anger, and misunderstanding. Unkindness causes you to view yourself and others as wrong or bad, and when that happens, you shut down your heart, because it seems as if love hurts too much. As a result you can feel isolated, fearful, and mistrustful, and engage in a painful cycle of feeling criticized, being critical of others, and putting a fortress around your heart. However, when your heart is open, you feel connected and experience life as precious. You may even sense that we're all inseparable expressions of one great unity.

A central question to inquire into is what prevents your heart from remaining open no matter what. To empower you, we look more deeply at nonviolence in more specific ways.

The Inner Voice of Criticism

The most prevalent form of violence takes place in your head, in the form of thoughts that shame, blame, judge, ridicule, attack, put down, discourage, and criticize you and others. These thoughts keep you anxious, distrustful, and defensive. This invisible and subtle form of violence tends to go unnoticed; however, its effect is similar to being physically attacked. A physical assault can be life threatening, and cause great pain and damage to your physical body, but regular doses of demeaning self-talk also beat you down. The toll of ongoing mental abuse is immense because it erodes your sense of basic goodness. You no longer experience your life as precious and don't feel safe, because you're mentally abusing yourself. The result is chronic fear and upset.

This form of violence can go on beneath your awareness. We live in a culture that not only tolerates but also seeks out violence in the news and entertainment media. Such continual exposure normalizes the images and sounds of violence. Most likely, your inner voice of criticism has been active for many years, and you've become so accustomed to it that you no longer recognize how it affects you.

Unknowingly, you may minimize the devastating effect of self-criticism. A silent form of verbal abuse, this form of violence reinforces old core stories of being flawed. Your cruel words to yourself have the same effect as when someone else says cruel and unkind things to you: internally you flinch, tighten, and feel emotionally unsafe. This process activates your body's fight-or-flight response.

PRACTICE: STOP THE VIOLENCE IN YOUR INNER WORLD

Nonviolence begins with becoming aware of your inner violence. Once you become aware of what harms you, then you can treat yourself more lovingly and begin healing your anxiety and suffering.

To begin, make a heading at the top of a piece of paper or a journal page titled "Words That Wound." List any and all words and phrases, such as "stupid" and "What's wrong with me, anyway?" that you silently say to yourself that scold, scorn, undermine, and reprimand you. Add to the list as more words come to mind. Make another heading titled "Words That Nurture." For every unkind word or phrase, write two kind ones, such as "Take it easy," "Yes, you can," "Breathe your way through it," and "It's okay." Build your vocabulary of words that nourish, encourage, and appreciate.

As you go about your days, listen to what you say to yourself. When you hear violent thoughts, stop and take a breath. Declare, "No more violence." Substitute a thought that proclaims your goodness, such as **Cherish this person** or **I love this person.**

Here's a little perspective. You wouldn't knowingly eat spoiled or toxic food, but if you accidentally did, you would spit it out as soon as you recognized it. Do the same with words; when you hear poisonous thoughts in your head, discharge them. Then breathe deeply to cleanse yourself, and select a life-affirming thought to counter the toxic one.

Sam's Story

Sam, the owner of a retail store, sought counseling for anxiety. He was riddled with worry about the well-being of his school-aged daughters. One day he told Mary about a murder story he saw on television earlier in the day and how he had then become consumed with fear that his daughters would be harmed on their way home from school. He added that he kept a news channel running at his store, which meant that he heard sensationalized news for nine hours a day, six days a week. In response to being bombarded with violence from the television, he was "entertaining" violence in his mind, conjuring up scenes about his daughters being hurt. He agreed to change to a sports channel immediately, and during a follow-up conversation two weeks later, he reported that his frantic worrisome thoughts had decreased. Since he no longer digested a diet of TV news and violence all day long, his preoccupation with the safety of his family had declined substantially.

Compassion

Another beneficial practice is to extend compassion to yourself. If you suffer from chronic anxiety, you need megadoses of understanding and encouragement to melt away your fear. While it's healing to receive kindness from others, it's truly transformational to receive kindness from yourself and to extend it to others.

When you look into the ways that violence lives in you, be very kind. Otherwise, as you become more aware of your self-critical words, you may unintentionally batter yourself by judging yourself harshly for being unable to stop thinking unkind thoughts, which in turn intensifies your anxiety. Treat yourself as compassionately as a loving grandmother kindly cares for her grandchildren.

PRACTICE: COMPASSIONATE CONVERSATION

This practice of compassion is a conversation within yourself, and takes the form of a compassionate response to your pain. If it helps you to access a voice of compassion, recall an older person who was kind to you. If none comes to mind, imagine what Jesus, Buddha, Mother Teresa, or another spiritual being would say to you. Remember or imagine how comforting it is to be understood. When you practice compassion, you're giving comfort and understanding to yourself.

Here's a compassionate response: "I give compassion to even this." Recite this response when you're being harsh with yourself. Rock, hug, and comfort yourself, whispering these words: "I give compassion to even this." These loving words touch your pain with kindness, and are powerfully healing.

Marjorie's Story

Marjorie had long been afraid that those she loved would leave her, just as her mother had done many years ago, when she was young. She hated the fact that she felt this way, and judged herself harshly for it, often crying out, "Why can't I get over this?" She berated herself for having such fear and wished it would go away. After mentally beating herself up, she felt bad about herself. At least, this is how it used to be. Now that she's aware of her fear and her violent reaction to it, she practices a compassion response. Here's a vignette of one conversation she had with herself:

> Fear: *I can't stop obsessing that my husband might be killed in a car accident. I'm so afraid that something will happen to him and I'll be left alone—geez, here I am, worrying again over nothing; I am so weak. I feel miserable.*

> Compassionate response: *Whoa, slow down—breathe. Let's be gentle; I give compassion to this fear.*

Fear: *I know, but I just can't stop worrying.*

Compassionate response: *Even this—I give compassion to even this.*

Fear: *What's wrong with me? I can't do this.*

Compassionate response: *Even this—I give compassion to even this.*

Gradually, she calmed down, took a few deep breaths and then spoke to herself in a nurturing way: *It's okay, it's okay.* Painfully aware of her fear of abandonment, she knows how rapidly self-critical talk escalates her anxiety. She has identified thoughts such as *I'm so weak* and *what's wrong with me* as violent, because they devalue her. Marjorie practices compassion when she falls into the cycle of intense fear followed by self-recrimination. Slowly, compassion is taking root as she responds to her pain with kindness; in her words, "I recover faster, and most of the time the fear doesn't escalate as it used to. It's so relieving to feel compassion. Now my fear is a form of suffering, not a big failure."

Truthfulness

The second principle is about being sincere and truthful. Consider how much you trust and admire people who have these qualities. They seem solid, reliable, and genuine; and you relax when you're around them, because you feel safe with them. And as you know, when you feel truly safe, you can express yourself, including your fears and difficulties. When you're around someone who's deceitful and withholding, you probably find it hard to relax. Most likely you feel leery, keep your distance, and don't show your vulnerability.

How we feel around others can help us learn more about how we feel around ourselves. When others are honest with you, you trust them more, and when *you* are honest with yourself, you trust

199

yourself more. You feel real rather than false in the way you do when you pretend, avoid, or deceive. Speaking truthfully is empowering, because when you tell the truth, you access its strength, which lessens the anxiety that stems from thinking you're "not competent enough." You may shake in your boots while challenging such lies, but you know deep down that you're being real.

Sorting Personal Truths

Personal truth has levels. Some are more transient and superficial, and others are deeper, more important, and act as motivators. For example, maybe you know you need to have a delicate conversation with a family member but are too tired, and fatigue increases your anxiety. If you're aware that you can breathe through your anxiety when you're rested, you'll postpone the discussion until the next morning. Being tired is a temporary reality, but the deeper truth is that the relationship truly matters and you want to be able to sort through the misunderstanding when you're rested, not exhausted.

Now let's say that you want to clear up a misunderstanding, but a more pervasive fear gets in the way. This fear acts as a motivator that causes you to avoid confrontations and let things slide. In this example, you have two personal truths: you're afraid, and you want to clear up a misunderstanding. Because fear is so powerful, you may rank it as more important than your desire to communicate with the people you love. However, it's not; fear isolates us and makes us suspicious. Communicating honestly with others connects us and makes us better able to trust. The first healing move is sorting out which personal truths matter the most. Two helpful questions to ask yourself are: "What really matters to me?" and "What's most important to me in this situation?"

PRACTICE: TELL THE TRUTH

When you're clearer about what's more important, it's time to practice telling the truth. Doing so will make you stronger. If underlying fear prevents you from taking part in confrontations, begin by acknowledging this out loud to yourself. Express your fear: "I want to speak up, but I'm afraid." Share this with someone else and write about it in your journal. Each time you express yourself, your ability to speak strengthens. Then, when you're strong enough, even if you're shaking in your boots, say, "I want to speak up, but I'm afraid," to the person you need to talk to. Actually speaking this truth will empower you to continue the conversation.

If you get to know your more central truths, fear will become less of a motivator. You may still feel anxious, but you can breathe your way through it. When your hands shake and your voice trembles, breathe and go step by step. Don't turn back, because you have more powerful motivators, such as love and your ongoing healing, to act on.

PRACTICE: ASK A GREAT QUESTION

There are times when you know something that you don't feel ready to know. The timing isn't right, you're afraid, it's inconvenient, it makes you uncomfortable, or you don't have the energy for it. Whatever the discomfort, you push what you know to be true to the side. But it's too late! Once you know the truth, you simply know. It's there, deep inside, working on you.

You know what we're referring to. This is the quiet, nagging truth that keeps popping up. It's the inner knowing that says, **The truth about this relationship is** _____, **I know I need to** _____, or **The real truth is** _____. Here's a wonderful question that helps you consciously acknowledge a truth that you know deep inside. Ask the question and listen. Wait for the answer.

What do I know about myself and my life that I haven't been listening to?

PRACTICE: INQUIRE INTO THE DATA

One way to counter anxiety is to do a reality check on your fear. Rather than automatically believe your fear, inquire. Investigate the data from the world outside of you:

- What's really going on here?

- What does the data say?

- What's the truth of the situation?

- What do I know for sure about this?

Inquire into your inner world of thinking by asking these questions:

- Is this belief true?

- Does the data substantiate my thinking?

- Am I in imminent danger?

Nonstealing

The meaning of this principle is straightforward: don't take what isn't yours. The most obvious interpretation of this principle is to avoid taking material things that aren't yours. In this discussion, we focus on the desire to be less like you and more like someone else. First of all, attempting to be like someone else is frustrating, because you're trying to copy something that you can't possibly duplicate, another person. Second, it causes anxiety, because you're trying to deprive yourself of being you. We can't take self-worth from another, and the only cause for wanting to do it is innocently believing the lie that you're not fundamentally okay. You've made mistakes; we all have. Good people make serious mistakes. You may have been deeply wounded and feel uncomfortable in your own skin. You may have lacked socioeconomic advantages and been unable to develop highly technical occupational skills. You may have been born with what your particular culture says is the wrong sex, the wrong skin color, or the wrong something else. However, none of this means that you're not worthy.

The thought *If only I could be like so-and-so* makes you feel miserable, less than the other person, and immobilized, because it's a denial of your own sacred value and potential. Being inspired by heroes and heroines has a different effect: you feel encouraged to take risks in spite of your fear. We don't heal anxiety by throwing our own lives away. We heal anxiety by becoming deeply involved in the fulfillment of our own lives.

PRACTICE: PRACTICE NONSTEALING

A powerful mantra for alleviating the desire to be someone else is "My essence is pure." This isn't to deny your problems but to help you avoid taking your mistakes, hurts, and lack of opportunities to be the sum total of who you are. You can't steal what's truly precious: self-worth, love, intelligence, contentment, and inner peace. Nor can you be less than what you are, which is why healing and true happiness depend on knowing and expressing your basic goodness.

Nonhoarding

Anxiety is fundamentally connected to mistrust, mistrusting the way life is, and mistrusting ourselves. One way we react to basic mistrust is by holding on to past experiences and stuff we no longer need. It's as if we try to create safety by stockpiling large amounts of food and clothing. This isn't to say that stockpiling isn't helpful at times. It is, such as when you buy extra groceries before a big snowstorm. Additionally, having a stash can give the confidence boost needed to start a new business or get out of an unhealthy relationship. However, there's no lasting security in holding on to unneeded stuff. Doing so only encumbers us. We know this at some level, yet hold on nonetheless, because we don't trust. Nonhoarding is the practice of releasing what's unnecessary or outlived.

Hanging on to unneeded possessions doesn't protect or insulate you from vulnerability or anxiety. We all have basic needs for our homes, families, health, and work, but beyond that, most possessions are optional. They provide neither safety nor happiness.

You don't become a more secure person by having more. When you rely on stuff to construct an identity or safety, over time it results in disappointment and anxiety. True confidence comes from recognizing that you're inherently sufficient, already whole as you are. Remember, you're living inside, and you're a manifestation, of God, consciousness, the great mystery, or however you describe it. You don't need to identify with something as finite as a possession.

PRACTICE: INQUIRE INTO HOARDING

Write the following self-inquiry questions in your journal and answer them as truthfully as you can:

- Which possessions do I truly need?

- What do I store and stockpile to make me feel secure?

- Which possessions do I use to build a sense of identity?

- What am I ready to let go of?

- What's my true source of security?

Gratitude and Nonhoarding

When fear is the motive behind accumulating, a deeper practice is useful. Being fearful makes you want to cling. And if you need to cling to your version of a good-luck charm, let it be; it's okay. Turn also to the goodness of life, even—and especially—when you've been hurt by life. Being thankful reminds you of life's goodness so that you don't fall into a fearful belief that life is all bad. Gratitude is the true practice of nonhoarding.

PRACTICE: CULTIVATE GRATITUDE

Make a daily list of appreciations. Write down five things each evening that you appreciated during the day. Nothing is too small to appreciate: a smile, a glimpse of nature, the absence of a headache. Especially appreciate the simple things. Give a prayer of gratitude each morning. Give thanks for the gift of life, little kindnesses, and lessons learned. Express thanks. Tell people that you're grateful they're in your life. Whisper, "Thank you," to your food, to the air you breathe, and to the floor you walk on.

ethical observances

These observances draw you more deeply into communion with higher consciousness. As such, they connect you to your divine essence and are the wellspring of inner peace. Then, when anxiety is happening on the outer surface, you don't feel as lost in it. On the surface you may shake with fear, but you know that deep inside you're sustained by a higher power.

Contentment

Contentment is a great virtue and a soothing balm for your anxious nerves. It's the ability to experience the joy of simply being while in the midst of doing. Described as having a foot in two worlds, contentment signifies being aware of the greater mystery while tending to the business of daily life. When you rock your baby and sense the presence of the sacred, you're contented. When you rock your baby and worry about paying bills, you're discontented. The task is the same; the experience is quite different.

You've met people who don't get lost in the frenzy. They see the bigger picture and take things in stride. They're easy to be with, and flow with life rather than resist it. This doesn't mean they're passive; they just don't argue with what is, including their emotions. If they feel afraid, they acknowledge their fear and move on. In fact, they're powerful because they direct their energy into dealing with life.

You hear them say, "It is what it is," not in resignation but with respect, sensing the greater mystery. This viewpoint allows them to make wise choices about how to spend their precious time and energy. Small things remain small, and ordinary living becomes enjoyable. As you can tell, anxiety dissolves in the presence of contentment.

PRACTICE: PRACTICE CONTENTMENT

Contentment is a very profound practice that creates samskaras of happiness. As a pattern, contentment is as easy to create as the habit of discontent. Here are a few ways to practice contentment. One is to find interesting, pleasant ways to do your tasks. Whenever possible, you may just as well enjoy what you're doing. When you're a little tense or upset, breathe in and out, and support yourself. Lift your arms over your head and stretch; take a big yawn. Doing so sounds ordinary, and is as mundane as stepping and breathing, but when you lift your arms up intentionally rather than absentmindedly, it's quite relieving.

Self-Discipline

Self-discipline refers to your resolve to do your daily yoga practices. It also includes adopting periodic practices, such as solitude and taking retreat. The result is that you strengthen your spiritual vitality. You've met or read about people who have spiritual radiance. Compassion, wisdom, and love of life emanate from them, and they inspire and heal you. This same spiritual fire is in you, however dim or bright it may be. Doing your practices fans this fire so that you feel its glow within you. This fire is what burns away the toxins, misunderstandings, and tensions that fuel your anxiety. If you submit to your yoga practices, your strength and vitality will grow.

PRACTICE: DEVELOP YOUR PERSONAL PRACTICE

Yoga practices don't help you unless you do them. So commit to doing a yoga practice that you actually want to do. Write it down, schedule it, and then follow through with it several times a week. Dedicate a specific period daily, and commit to your practice. Begin where you are, start small, and go step by step. Your practice doesn't have to be long and grueling to be beneficial, but you do have to show up for your appointment with yoga. Here's a sample schedule for a daily yoga practice:

1. Schedule thirty minutes for your practice and go to a quiet room.

2. Begin with a devotional reading from a sacred text.

3. Sit quietly for a couple of minutes and contemplate the reading.

4. Do fifteen minutes of gentle yoga poses (warm up with the bridge-pose flow and the five easy poses; see chapter 6).

5. Sit comfortably and practice breath awareness for a couple of minutes.

6. Meditate or recite your mantra for ten minutes or more.

Surrender to God or Ultimate Reality

This observance connotes submission to ultimate reality, just what's needed, though at times hard to do when we're moderately anxious and trying to hold ourselves together. The observance of worship and devotion, this is about laying our lives, our problems, and our successes at the feet of the great mystery. When you say, "Thy will, not my will," you're submitting to a higher power and practicing this observance.

This process is also about intimacy, the kind that grows out of experience. You may know what it's like to turn to the divine in desperation. In great pain, when all your efforts to hold yourself and your life together fail, you fall to the floor and cry out. Your cries are a way of letting go of what you can't understand or control. You just know you're overwhelmed and have to surrender. While praying, you feel miserably alone, yet somehow comforted and not alone. It may not be easy to turn to what you can't see or understand, yet when you do, you make a life-changing discovery. You realize that getting your way doesn't grow faith, but feeling the support, strength, and palpable aliveness of ultimate reality does.

PRACTICE: YOUR PERSONAL PRACTICE OF SURRENDER

There's no one way to practice. Do what most touches you and appeals to you. Look at the stars in the night sky, and know that you're in the presence of vastness. Lie on the floor and breathe. Write devotional poems. Bow down in humility. Credit it all to God.

conclusion

When you take them into your heart and your life, these principles and observances are sources of strength and kindness.

As guidelines, they show you how to center your life around truth and kindness. When you fall, they help you get back up, and aid you in accepting your humanity. The result is that you live more peacefully amid others, experience the extraordinary in the ordinary, and live as though you're a manifestation of the divine, which you are.

conclusion

$h$ere, at the end of the book, you're where you were when you first began reading it: in the present moment, still going step by step, breath by breath. Only now, if you've been practicing, you're more conscious of what you're doing. Whether or not you're aware of it, seeds of great possibility have been planted in you—by you—that sooner or later will germinate into new life. They're in your sanka-lpa resolutions (see chapter 5), nurturing self-talk, and mantra practice. You make space for them to grow each time you hear those old stories and whisper, "Innocent misunderstanding." You tend to them lovingly whenever you give yourself time to be silent and listen deeply.

You've learned:

- To breathe and steady yourself through waves of anxiety

- A gentle practice of physical postures to comfort your body and open your heart

- Compassionate listening to melt the pain of self-destructive behaviors

- An inner knowing, that you're whole and truly precious

You may temporarily forget about your inner essence, but you can remember again. Turn to your memories of mystical experiences and those occasions when you felt deeply connected. The peace that pervaded those experiences is not bounded by time, and you can, once again, be aware of the still, loving presence you felt then, for it's always within you.

As you go about your life, know that your practices are transforming you. You may already find that your anxiety isn't as intense or that things that previously stopped you in your tracks don't bother you as much. You may also be discovering that it's now easier being you. Be faithful to your practices; let them sustain you moment by moment by moment. You'll reap the benefits and start to see changes occurring. Growth is challenging, but you have your companions of breathing and witnessing to strengthen and support you.

You may also be discovering that the stuff of great suffering—unfortunate things that happened, worries you carried for years, and all that painful self-talk that brought you to these yoga practices—now helps you to know your essence and your loving heart. Life is mysterious in that our difficulties are also our teachers. If we embrace everything that happens, then it may be that the anguish of our anxiety actually helps us to discover what beautiful, spiritual beings we are. And once we know the truth, we become incapable of perpetuating the damaging patterns that cause pain to ourselves and others. Perhaps this is the way that our healing from anxiety brings joy and decency into the world around us.

references

Benson, H. 1976. *The Relaxation Response.* New York: HarperTorch.

Brefczynski-Lewis, J. A., A. Lutz, H. S. Schaefer, D. B. Levinson, and R. J. Davidson. 2007. Neural correlates of attentional expertise in long-term meditation practitioners. *Proceedings of the National Academy of Sciences* 104 (27):11483–88.

Cannon, W. 1915. *Bodily Changes in Pain, Hunger, Fear and Rage: An Account of Recent Researches into the Function of Emotional Excitement.* New York: Appleton and Company.

Desikachar, T. K. V. 1999. *The Heart of Yoga: Developing a Personal Practice.* Rochester, VT: Inner Traditions International.

Eriksson, P. S., E. Perfilieva, T. Björk-Eriksson, A.M. Alborn, C. Nordborg, D. A. Peterson, and F. H. Gage. 1998. Neurogenesis in the adult human hippocampus. *Nature Medicine* 4:1313–17.

Felitti, V. J., R. F. Anda, D. Nordenberg, D. F. Williamson, A. M. Spitz, V. Edwards, M. P. Koss, and J. S. Marks. 1998. Relationship of childhood abuse and household dysfunction to many of the leading causes of death in adults: The Adverse Childhood Experiences (ACE) Study. *American Journal of Preventive Medicine* 14 (4):245–58.

Feuerstein, G. 1998. *The Yoga Tradition: Its History, Literature, Philosophy, and Practice.* Prescott, AZ: Hohm Press.

Forbes, B. 2004. Stuck in a rut. *Yoga Journal* August.

Forbes, B., C. Akturk, C. Cummer-Nacco, P. Gaither, J. Gotz, A. Harper, and K. Hartsell. 2008. Yoga therapy in practice: Using integrative yoga therapeutics in the treatment of comorbid anxiety and depression. *International Journal of Yoga Therapy* Vol. 18:87–95.

Green, E., and A. Green. 1977. *Beyond Biofeedback.* New York: Delacorte Press/Seymour Lawrence.

Iyengar, B. K. S. 1993. *Light on the Yoga Sūtras of Patañjali.* San Francisco: HarperCollins Publishers.

Kabat-Zinn, J., A. Chapman, and P. Salmon. 1997. The relationship of cognitive and somatic components of anxiety to patient preference for alternative relaxation techniques. *Mind/Body Medicine* 2:101–09.

Kasamatsu, A., and T. Hirai. 1966. An electroencephalographic study on the Zen meditation (zazen). *Folia psychiatrica et neurologica Japonica* 20 (4):315–36.

Kessler, R. C., W. T. Chiu, O. Demler, and E. E. Walters. 2005. Prevalence, severity, and comorbidity of 12-month DSM-IV disorders in the National Comorbidity Survey Replication. *Archives of General Psychiatry* 62 (6):617–27.

Kraftsow, G. 2002. *Yoga for Transformation: Ancient Teachings and Practices for Healing the Body, Mind, and Heart.* New York: Penguin Compass.

Lasater, J. 1995. *Relax and Renew: Restful Yoga for Stressful Times.* Berkeley, CA: Rodmell Press.

Lazar, S. W., C. E. Kerr, R. H. Wasserman, J. R. Gray, D. N. Greve, M. T. Treadway, M. McGarvey, B. T. Quinn, J. A. Dusek, H. Benson, S. L. Rauch, C. I. Moore, and B. Fischl. 2005. Meditation experience is associated with increased cortical thickness. *Neuroreport* 16 (17):1893–97.

LeDoux, J. 1998. *The Emotional Brain: The Mysterious Underpinnings of Emotional Life.* New York: Simon and Schuster.

———. 2007. Emotional memory. *Scholarpedia* 2 (7):1806.

Lutz, A., L. L. Greischar, N. B. Rawlings, M. Ricard, and R. J. Davidson. 2004. Long-term meditators self-induce high-amplitude gamma synchrony during mental practice. *Proceedings of the National Academy of Sciences* 101 (46):16369–73.

Mallinger, A. E., and J. DeWyze. 1992. *Too Perfect: When Being in Control Gets Out of Control.* New York: Fawcett Columbine.

McCall, T. 2007. *Yoga as Medicine: The Yogic Prescription for Health and Healing.* New York: Bantam Books.

Murphy, M. 1999. Scientific studies of contemplative experiences: An overview. In *The physical and psychological effects of meditation: A review of contemporary research with a comprehensive bibliography, 1931–1996,* 2nd ed., M. Murphy and S. Donovan, ed. E. Taylor. Petaluma, CA: Institute of Noetic Sciences.

Pearce, J. C. 2002. *The Biology of Transcendence: A Blueprint of the Human Spirit*. Rochester, VT: Inner Traditions International.

Sapolsky, R. M. 2004. *Why Zebras Don't Get Ulcers*. New York: Henry Holt and Company.

Schwartz, J. M., and S. Begley. 2002. *The Mind and the Brain: Neuroplasticity and the Power of Mental Force*. New York: HarperCollins Publishers.

Stiles, M. 2002. *Yoga Sutras of Patanjali*. Boston: Red Wheel/ Weiser.

Swami Durgananda. 2002. *The Heart of Meditation: Pathways to a Deeper Experience*. South Fallsburg, New York: Siddha Yoga Publications.

Swami Rama. 1988. *Path of Fire and Light*. Vol. 2. Honesdale, PA: The Himalayan Institute Press.

Swami Rama, R. Ballentine, and Swami Ajaya. 1976. *Yoga and Psychotherapy: The Evolution of Consciousness*. Honesdale, PA: Himalayan International Institute.

Van der Kolk, B. 2006. Clinical implications of neuroscience research in PTSD. In *Psychobiology of posttraumatic stress disorder: A decade of progress*, ed. R. Yehuda. New York: New York Academy of Sciences.

Mary NurrieStearns, LCSW, RYT, is a psychotherapist and yoga teacher with a counseling practice in Tulsa, OK. She is author of numerous articles on psychospiritual growth and coeditor of the book *Soulful Living*. She has also produced audio CDs on yoga and meditation as healing practices. She teaches yoga, mindfulness, and meditation, leads transformational meditation and yoga retreats, and teaches seminars across the United States.

Rick NurrieStearns is a meditation teacher, coeditor of the book *Soulful Living*, and was the publisher of *Personal Transformation*, a magazine on psychospiritual growth. He has been immersed in consciousness studies for more than thirty-five years, working with the country's leading authors and healers in transpersonal psychology. With Mary, he leads transformational meditation and yoga retreats.

Visit the NurrieStearnses online at www.PersonalTransformation .com.

Photographer **Kim Shetter** practices yoga and photography in northern California.

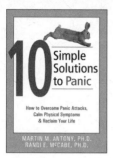
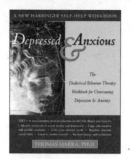

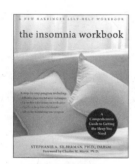